"As Scott Gould's brilliantly titled memoir indicates, this is the very territory of this book: the relationship between the blast-radius and transcendence. In a curious sense, they are synonymous. No crashes; no flights. With truly impressive distance and irony, Gould takes his own set of tragic circumstances and turns them into nothing less than an allegory of the cost of being fully human and vulnerable. An extraordinary work."
DAVID SHIELDS, AUTHOR OF
THE THING ABOUT LIFE IS THAT ONE DAY YOU'LL BE DEAD

"In his masterful memoir, *Things That Crash, Things That Fly*, Scott Gould navigates seamlessly between dark-comic wit and bare-knuckled heartbreak, guiding the reader through a crisis of spirit that is at once singular and universal. Gould's talents as a celebrated fiction writer animate these pages, each brief chapter perfectly calibrated to propel the story forward. Every character, even the most minor, bristles with life. As the title suggests, even things that crash—a WWII plane in the Italian countryside, a marriage of nearly two decades, unrealized dreams—can be resurrected in new forms. And if the past is haunted by ghosts, the future is alive with the possibility of angels."
REBECCA MCCLANAHAN, AUTHOR OF
IN THE KEY OF NEW YORK CITY: A MEMOIR IN ESSAYS

"I love everything about this book, but two things most: the going-for-broke honesty and the great good humor with which this tale of heartbreak is told. Scott Gould is a born storyteller, and gives here the story he was born to give: his own loss that begins in a South Carolina kitchen, then the dark vacation of the soul he must make it through thereafter, then his own walkabout among the good people of Italy and the awful history of war in order to find his own heart returned to him, not unscathed but stronger for all it's been through. Read this book. You'll be a better person for it. And you'll have a good time too."
BRET LOTT, AUTHOR OF *JEWEL*

"Interwoven with the story of the young WWII pilot who falls from the sky into a small Tuscan village, Scott Gould's captivating memoir straddles two worlds as he plots a course through his own fall and does so with such hard-won and gorgeous truth-telling, you'll cheer him as he lands."

SONJA LIVINGSTON, AUTHOR OF *GHOSTBREAD*

About the Author

Scott Gould is the author of the story collection, *Strangers to Temptation* (Hub City Press), and the novels, *Whereabouts* (Koehler Books) and *The Hammerhead Chronicles* (University of North Georgia Press). His work has appeared in *Kenyon Review, Black Warrior Review, New Ohio Review, Crazyhorse, Carolina Quarterly, New Stories from the South* and others. He is a multiple winner of the Individual Artist Fellowship in Prose from the South Carolina Arts Commission, as well as the Fiction Fellowship from the South Carolina Academy of Authors. He lives in Sans Souci, South Carolina.

More information is available at
www.scottgouldwriter.com

Things That Crash,

Things That Fly

Scott Gould

Vine Leaves Press
Melbourne, Vic, Australia

Things That Crash, Things That Fly
Copyright © 2021 Scott Gould
All rights reserved.

Print Edition
ISBN: 978-1-925965-46-9
Published by Vine Leaves Press 2021
Melbourne, Victoria, Australia

Cover design by Jessica Bell
Cover images by © Alex © wrongorright © Yulia © msokolyan
Interior design by Amie McCracken

A catalogue record for this
book is available from the
National Library of Australia

To the people of Serra,
who provide places to land

And in memory of Antonluigi Aiazzi

Author's Note

This is a memoir, a story based on experience and memory. The author has attempted to re-create events, locations and dialogue as accurately as possible from his recollections and notes. The book is, ultimately, the author's truth, as he remembers it.

Table of Contents

A PROLOGUE

I am six-foot-three and my hairline is hauling ass.
I am not fond of small, yippy dogs. I hate back hair—mine, I mean—so every few months I go to a spa that smells like patchouli and cinnamon and a large, whispering woman who used to wax porn stars in Los Angeles rips the epidermis from my shoulder blades. I like her. She's a good storyteller and doesn't even realize it.

I have a big ugly scar on the right side of my left knee because I possess bad juju with that particular joint. Hair again: I shave my legs because my cycling buddies made fun of me at a stop sign one morning. That is all I will say about hair.

I drink Pabst Blue Ribbon beer and collect the bottle caps because playing card values appear on the undersides—the numbers and suits and face cards. This is the only collection I have.

I shoot squirrels from my back window with a Remington pellet gun I bought at Wal-Mart. I cook quesadillas and pork loin, but not simultaneously. I eat out too much.

I drive a car that belonged to my father, which sounds lame until you realize that everything he owns lasts forever. It's a 2001 Pontiac Bonneville. A Bonneville—I cringe to tell you that. What's left of the hair on my head, I have buzzed at Great Clips for $8 if I get there before nine in the morning for the discount. (Sorry, more hair.)

I am cheap, but a woman I used to know once called me a shoe whore. I will drop several large bills on a pair of shoes. I do not believe shoes make the man but a pair of leather, hand-tooled sandals from Italy can make everyone forget your jeans are from Old Navy. (Smoke and mirrors, my friend, smoke and mirrors.)

I played college basketball. I got good grades. I think hockey is confusing. I worry that my father has bequeathed me his lemon-sized prostate. I always cry during the final scene of *Cinema Paradiso*. I have two daughters who like me, at least that's what they say, and I possess only a meager estate to leave them, so they have no real motivation to feign affection.

So much more, of course. But here's the point: I will tell you anything you want to know.

I.
WHAT THE WRENS HEARD

1.

It happens in the kitchen.

Usually good things happen there. The history of this kitchen is no different. It's long and wide, so long I had room to put a heavy, wooden table in the back half. When people visit, they linger around that table. I floored the kitchen with hardwoods because I'd never seen one with wooden floors, always cold, hard tile or cheesy linoleum. She thinks I am crazy, but she ends up liking it. She is an ex-dancer, which is why she always seems to be barefoot. She enjoys feeling the ground directly beneath the soles of her splayed out feet.

Outside the kitchen window stands a pergola I built one Mother's Day weekend. The pergola was a gift to my wife, an homage to her Italian heritage. Truthfully, it took me several weekends to finish. I'm not a very skilled carpenter, and I've never been good at squaring the corners of anything, so I had to restart a couple of times to avoid building a pergola shaped like a parallelogram. I planted Crossvine the evening I finally finished, one small, insignificant plant at the base of each support post. By now, the treated four-by-fours and beams have weathered to a nice gray color and are smothered with a thick canopy of green shade we use almost every night, once the weather turns in April or so. Wrens nest in the pergola this time of year, among the vines. I have to clean wren crap off the Plexiglas table every couple of days.

A coating of yellow-green powder dusts the window sill and the window frame. It is early spring in South Carolina. I've endured plodding, monotonous sinus headaches from allergies for a solid week, and I should offer to wash the windows, but really, who washes windows these days?

We stand in the kitchen talking about this trip we can't afford to take. We are not the type of people who can simply jet off to Italy. Those people drive different cars than ours. Their credit cards are a different color. I can't imagine how much this trip will ultimately cost. I want to talk about how to get around Italy cheaply. But conversations like that make her scowl. She's never enjoyed the sound of me squeezing our nickels.

And I want to talk logistics. I want to make sure my parents know what day to come up and move into the spare room. I want to talk about how it makes more sense to rent a tiny, cramped Fiat, so we can save on gas money. The look on her face hasn't changed. A cloud has risen there, swirling behind the eyes, her perfect brown eyes, the eyes she gave to both of our daughters.

I'm tired of thinking about money. I want to sit under the pergola and have a beer and listen to the traffic begin to thin on the street behind our house. I don't like planning. I'm a lazy man. Ok, I think, just give in. Rent the bigger car. In the long run, it's not that much money. Yes, I will tell her, you can ship back as much olive oil as you want. You can buy more dishes to match the ones you bought the last trip to Italy. I'll only buy one pair of shoes.

Her eyes haven't moved off of me. The cloud isn't clearing. She sits on a barstool and looks away from where I stand in our kitchen. The smell of the tuna casserole lingers from dinner. The oven pings as it cools down. She takes a breath, and then she says it. She says when we get back from Italy, after our trip is over and done, she is leaving me. Moving out.

Such small words filling the air and fluttering like nervous birds searching for places to land. Another story for this kitchen, the newest memory. Then the cloud breaks behind her eyes and she begins to cry, which means, I suppose, that she is serious, that starting now, this is real.

2.

The perfect magic trick. You study the magician carefully, trying to detect a flaw, a slight hiccup in her sleight-of-hand, but no matter how closely you stalk the flights of her fingers, you spot nothing out of place. Those fingers are insects—buzzing, moving and darting, never landing. She drapes a red cloth over the small chicken crammed in a small cage and chants a couple of incantations, and you find yourself predicting, wanting to stay ahead of the magician, and she suddenly snatches the cape from the pedestal. There, in front of you is something you never expected, even with your wildest predictions. An albino snake or a canned ham. A goldfish bowl with a canary in it. The perfect trick. Something that came out of the blue and smacked you between the eyes.

Standing there in the kitchen, like an audience member in the front row, I am awestruck, trying to unravel the trick this magician just pulled on me.

3

I did not see this coming.

Sure, sure, *now* when I glance back I spot signs. I see bright, fluorescent tracers zipping at me from the edge of the marital jungle, but back *then* I didn't notice the danger. I've always been a grinder. Settling in for the long haul. We have been married seventeen years. Twenty is just around the corner. Then fifty. Then matching cremation urns on a daughter's mantel. She is not a grinder. I've always known this, but I thought I could grind enough for the both of us, shoulder us through whatever inclines we hit, pump the brakes on the down slopes.

She is leaving, she says. In the cause-and-effect equation that is our lives, she is always cause. A magician. Me, I'm effect. I am the one who watches the magic act unfold and gets surprised in the end. Tonight I am surprised.

She remains seated, her perfect dancer's posture on the barstool. Perhaps she is afraid if she stood, she might walk away too soon, before we even board a plane for Italy. She might actually run off into the night. *I need some time*, she says. *I need some space to think*. She's lived with me long enough to know how much I despise clichés. I want to grab a red marker and bracket what she just said and take off twenty points for hackneyed language and piss-poor excuses for bailing on a marriage.

More sentences tumble out of her, and I hear the tinny echo of rehearsal. This isn't the first time she's said them. They are too polished, too practiced. I know her. She probably wrote all this down. She is always writing down things so she won't forget them or won't mess them up. She loves her lists. This sounds like a speech, especially the part when she talks about passion. *You have lost your passion*, she says. And I want to laugh because I feel like I have stepped into a sappy cable TV movie. She will finish this speech, and we will cut to a commercial before my response.

That's right, she says, pointing at me—and even the gesture is too big, too rehearsed. *You've lost your passion. I have to have the passion every day.*

I'm not sure what daily passion means. Is it like a vitamin and you need a minimum daily requirement? Does daily passion mean she wants to have sex every day? Or argue every day? Or argue and cap it off with sex? Every single day? I need definitions, guidelines. I'm that kind of person. But I suppose I shouldn't have to talk about it. One should just know passion by sight, or be able to recognize it in the dark. Right?

She waits for me to respond, and I want to hear more. (Maybe if I keep her talking, she can never leave.) She says—after my silence hangs in the air like a bad odor—*See what I mean? Exactly. You can't even talk about it. No passion.*

She's right, of course. I'm chicken shit. I couldn't bring my questions to the surface, where they could actually be heard. Probably because I'm afraid of the answer. Instead, I look around the room and notice all of the mistakes. Where I cut the hardwood boards too short on the floor, just under the cabinet's edge. The bad paint job around the edges of that one switch plate. The uneven oven eye that tips pots to one side.

She checks the clock. Odd that she's worried about the time right now.

I would think—I would hope—if I was going to leave someone, I'd have the good sense to come up with an original reason. But maybe there isn't one. Maybe all the good ones have been used and turned into clichés.

I mean, she's the ex-dancer. She likes the safety of movement. For her, leaving is, perhaps, simply new choreography.

4.

I wonder why my first thought isn't to talk her out of her decision. Maybe her rehearsed lines convince me instantly it would be useless. Maybe I don't have the energy or the balls.

No, the first thought that flies into my head is about the girls. They will hate us for this. For the rest of their lives, my daughters will point at the scars I helped create—the same way I point at my mangled knee—and say, *This is what they did to me. It never healed properly.*

This is my first thought.

5.

The oldest daughter (call her E) is a tiny, tiny girl. She is sixteen. She is, officially, a Little Person. Before she was even born, the doctors came to us and announced she was the possessor of a Random Gene Mutation. We got a call late one afternoon, confirming the suspicions and the measurements. Her mother and I stood in the hallway of our brick rental house near Poinsett Highway, a block behind the gem-and-rock shop. The house smelled like bacon until we pulled up the ancient shag carpets that had been saturated for decades with the clouds from greasy breakfasts. Under the carpets, perfect hardwoods. We felt lucky for discovering them. We felt lucky about most things those days.

When the doctor hung up, we both sank in the hallway, slid down the wall and looked at each other. I would have to help her back to her feet, her belly too full to rise easily. Until then, I'd never lived in a precise moment I knew life had changed, but this was one. Like suddenly being struck deaf or blind, I was missing any sense of direction. She cried first, there on the floor.

Doctors are often painfully callous, especially when it comes to giving news that nobody wants to hear. I hated the word *random* he'd kept using on the phone. There was nothing random about it. It was very non-random. It was an unbelievably specific son of a bitch. Everything but E's arms and legs grew. Everything including her attitude. When she was old enough, she was a prime candidate—with those little bitty arms and legs and that tornado attitude—for limb-lengthening surgeries. All that metal, all that pain.

She took it on and stretched her Random Gene Mutation a solid eleven inches. She's a shade under five feet tall now and keeps her middle finger hiked at the world most of the time.

The younger one (call her M) did laps in the parental gene pool and avoided randomness and inherited her mother and father's length. She is thirteen now. She is turning willowy as the days pass. Willowy and blonde. She was born long and thin and screaming, big round eyes wide open, but that was the last time she tried to upset anyone else's silence. She is too kind for her own good, all of her nerve endings pulsing just under the surface of her thin skin. She is hurt too quick and too often. She possesses an overabundance of guilt not just for the things she's done, but for the things she's merely contemplated. And she is chock full of anxiety. E doesn't have anxiety. She doesn't worry about anything. Her pulse rate hovers just above comatose. M, though, wakes up worrying. Combined, the two of them have ample height and a perfectly balanced psyche. Break them apart and they need shoe lifts and Zoloft and a referee. I adore them as a team. I love them solo.

When E was young and in the midst of her limb-lengthening surgeries, she and her mother would live in Northern Virginia for months at a time to be near doctors and physical therapists. Every other Friday, M and I would drive north to see them for the weekend. We left in the late afternoons, after work, and before we crossed into North Carolina, we would be speeding through the falling dark. M offered to sing to keep me awake. She was in her country music phase. We drove into the night, into that time warp that comes from driving after sundown, knowing the next time you see daylight, you'll be in a different state, a different bed.

She sang along to the radio, country song after country song after country song. We would listen to a couple dozen tunes until the FM station faded, then dial up another station broadcasting the same exact playlist. I forgot about the miles, listening to M sing. Her pitch was nearly perfect, even though she was so young she had to be strapped in a car seat. She would fade to sleep some time into the night, after dinner, her voice trailing off in the middle of a song about love gone bad or bad love finally gone.

The next time she woke, she would be curled up next to her sister, or at least as close as she could get. E wore a shiny contraption of metal and wire on her legs—intricate, complicated circles that resembled miniature Ferris wheels. We all kept our distance from her bare, lengthening legs. The two girls would lie next to each other, the worrier and the patient, and I would lie nearby, next to their mother, the four of us wrapped up in whatever we could find to throw over our shoulders to keep us all warm.

6.

My second thought brings on that warm wash of relief you experience when you wake from a nightmare and realize it was only a crappy dream. I am suddenly The World's Most Logical Man. I look at her crying. She avoids my eyes. I tell her: *Well, then we're not going to Italy, obviously. If we never go there, you can't leave me when we come back!*

I am brilliant.

I stand as tall as I can, the classic redneck intimidation technique. I give her the perfect look, the one that tells her everything without making a sound, one that says: *We will stay here and ferret out the problems you are having with yourself and with me. We will find where the pain is coming from and we will get rid of it.*

I will teach her how to be a grinder. I will show her there are always good times on the other side of the bad, if you just push through. Glances in the rearview mirror never seemed like a sane way to repair bad situations. I'm a muddler *and* a grinder. I muddle through to the other side. I will carry burdens as long as it takes to move them from one place to the other. That's probably why I have bad knees.

So, I think, we can just stay at home and work on modern solutions, solutions that not only make her happy but make us stronger in the process. This plan feels like glue. We will epoxy our marriage. I smile, and she continues to cry.

She dismisses the idea with a wave of her hand. When she finally speaks, she says *we have no choice but to go to Italy*. She demands we go. *We've paid deposits, invited friends, coordinated relatives to watch the kids.* She says, *we can't tell anyone anything about this. You have to promise not to tell anyone. It will ruin their trip.*

Her instructions sound rehearsed as well, like she's known for days, weeks maybe, that this moment was coming. We are to act as if nothing is wrong in front of our friends. We don't want to be a bad influence, a bad omen. It will be the little carry-on bag packed with quiet shame that we carry to Italy.

I can't be responsible for ruining their vacation, she says.

She's worried more about people we see a half dozen times a year than she is about me, than she is about our daughters. This is a revelation, this concern for random friends. It means something. I'm not sure what.

So there, in the kitchen, I agree to everything. To the trip. To the silence. To the smiles I will be forced to flash at people who have rock-solid marriages. I don't care about them. I don't care about money either. There is no way to sit down and calculate what this is going to cost. We'll rent a Mercedes. Doesn't matter. I don't care about anything except stopping her crying. I try to imagine trudging through another country, carrying this around. I grab the sides of the counter for some balance and find something old and sticky under my fingers, something the kids left there months, maybe years, ago—a surprise. The kids. Now I want to cry. They won't have the benefit of seeing this barreling down on them.

The kids, I say.

After the trip, she says back.

Everything is *after* this trip. Life begins after this trip. That's what she thinks. This trip, for her, is a palate cleanser. Something to get rid of the taste in her mouth. I look at the pollen again on the window. There's not a chance of rain for another week or so, and then only a slight one. We're in the midst of a bad drought. Of course we are, I think.

She finally stands up and throws her shoulders back. She has wide shoulders, swimmer's shoulders, and they are brown from working in the yard. In front of me, she fills her lungs and sighs, her feet splayed into first position on the hardwood. She is just out of my reach. I can't possibly grab her shoulders and pull her in.

7.

I have another idea in the kitchen.

When I was young, before my knee joint disintegrated, I played basketball for hours a day. I was a gym rat with a smooth, steady jump shot that compensated for being slow and unable to elevate. Because I was slow, I had to be a smart basketball player. I could figure out how to beat someone because I kept my eyes open, looking for weaknesses, for tips, for tells. I always assumed the guy bellying up to me, trying to keep me from the hoop, didn't have a brain like mine. I eventually played college ball, banging people around with my brain, until my left knee finally gave out. And I hated losing. During games, I enjoyed the fact that there was always a fourth quarter or a few ticks left on the clock to pull out a win. I thought: if I have enough time, I can figure out a way to win.

So I think: I can pull this off in Italy. There is plenty of time left on the clock. I can save it. I can hit a shot just before the buzzer goes off. She's made a strategic error; she's left me with too much time. I can figure out a way to win this back. I want the ball in my hands this time. The clock is ticking.

I decide to surprise her. So I smile. (I can tell she isn't expecting it.) I smile and say, *Okay then, let's go to Italy*, and her eyes go a bit cloudy with confusion. I don't believe she thought it would be this easy to get exactly what she wants. But I have plans. Game plans.

8.

Where she goes after she leaves the kitchen, I can't say. Maybe down the long hallway to the bedroom or to the den so she can stare at the television. (I hear it playing. The girls are watching some show that is loud with music.) Our house is big, a single story ranch-style built in the 1960s. Sounds tend to flow down the long hallway. And there are plenty of places to hide.

I grab a beer from the refrigerator and head outside to the pergola. Underneath the umbrella of Crossvine, the air is thick enough to grab. It smells like grass and dust. We need a good rain to settle everything. I sit at the table, and the mosquitoes find me quickly, buzzing my ears. I am suddenly too tired to bat at them, too tired to even find a book of matches and light the citronella candles. It's easier to let them annoy me.

My knee, the one that's been operated on a half-dozen times, aches. It doesn't usually hurt like this until I strain it, push it too hard, like the weekend I carried all the four-by-four beams for the pergola from the driveway to the back-yard. Tonight, it just hurts out of spite. I can't get comfortable in my chair. I think of things I could have said. I should have asked her, *Why now? Why not wait and tell me after the trip?*

The sound over my head—something incessant and panicked, a manic rustling in the Crossvine canopy. It's the wrens. Though I was trying to be quiet, I've made too much noise, upset their evening. They will have trouble settling back in their roosts. I don't know how I'm going to get through the coming weeks. I have a mantra I've always used with my daughters. I tell them: *Never worry about something until you have something to worry about.*

Now, I have something to worry about, something large and looming, and all I can think about is how those goddamn wrens are going to be up all night. Maybe this is what it feels like the first day you're completely lost.

9.

I talk too much about my knee. But when something attached to you is a source of constant pain, you can't help yourself. I always wondered why my father yammered on about his prostate or my uncle made his hammertoe the subject of dinner conversation. Now I know. It feels better to talk about pain that won't go away.

In high school, one morning during a full-court scrimmage, something clicked in my left knee. Subtle, like someone depressed the end of a ballpoint pen. The tiny click leveled me on the floor. A few hours later, I was in an orthopedist's office, staring at x-rays that showed a couple nickel-sized pieces of bone that had broken off in my joint, pieces currently floating around in that tiny space until I tried to take a step, when they lodged in the joint. Hence, the lightning.

The next morning, the orthopedist operated. They gave me spinal anesthesia, which meant I could hear everything going on around me. I heard the doctor ask for nails and a hammer. Next, I heard the *tink, tink* of the hammer on the tiny nail and felt a shudder ripple up my legs all the way to my head. He had a plan. He nailed the chunks of bone (technically the condyles) back into place. I'd be on crutches for three months or so. Then he'd go back in and take the nails out. Hopefully, the bone would re-attach and adhere, good as new. A few more weeks on crutches after that, and I'd be back on the court.

And I was. The plan worked. At least for a couple of years. The bones broke away again when I played in college. He repeated the process. In between, there were a couple of reconnaissance missions into the joint with an arthroscope to see what was going on. A grand total of six surgeries.

This was a long time ago. Orthopedists back then didn't seem to worry too much about destroying cartilage when they were asking for their hammer and nails. My cartilage, what little was left, dissolved over the years. So now I have a knee that crunches all day. More lightning when I sit down or stand up. The thought of dragging myself around Italy already hurts. I've tried everything. Drugs. Trips to Atlanta where some doctor for the Falcons wanted to sign me up for an experiment that involved cadaver cartilage. (I wanted to do that one just so I would have a story. It never happened.) Nothing has worked. It always hurts. And I talk about it too much.

So that's the knee thing.

10.

We act like normal people preparing for a normal trip.

I huddle over a map unfolded across the kitchen table, trace future days in Italy with an index finger sliding across the colors, along the highways and contours of the hills. Once she looks over my shoulder at the map and makes a noise, sort of a *harrumph*. (There are blankets of silence and so little talking that I begin to count the noises she makes.) We buy new shoes, with actual arches built for walking up hills and through museums. We get new toothbrushes or fill prescriptions that might run out while we're gone. We lay separate suitcases on the bed, but we don't discuss who should pack what. We are not sharing that space anymore. We look at each other as little as possible.

We just let the day come.

For me, that day is the start of the fourth quarter of this game. It's when I am going to save things. I stock up on Ibuprofen for my barking knee, which seems to be getting worse, and the bone-on-bone pain is making stairs—especially going down them—a new experience in wincing. But I will play through this particular discomfort. I will eat Ibuprofen like Tic Tacs. I will grit my teeth. I have no plan for the pain. I don't really have a plan for anything. I am going to rely on instincts.

It would be completely fair to say that operating without a plan, that relying only on instincts, had blazed the current shit-soaked path that led to my present predicament, but that would be a mistake. Just the opposite, in fact. My instincts have been on sabbatical, I believe. Not keeping watch. Not practicing vigilance. Now, they will resurface and lead me through the fourth quarter, ball in my hand, time running down. The only commandment in the No-Plan Plan is to constantly occupy a place in her field of vision when I need to be seen, and to be conspicuously absent if I sense she needs—how was it she put it?—*space to think.*

For her, I suppose the day of our departure will be a confusing mixture of elements, the ultimate emotional conundrum. It is the beginning of the end of her beginning, some sort of circular, snake-eating-its-tail time warp. The idea of getting through customs will take on a new significance in her mind. I can see her contemplating leaving the States as one sort of citizen, and returning as a stranger in a new land. She, at least as I imagine it, will come home a foreigner. Unless of course, I change everything before time winds down.

So I keep my mouth shut, the twin anvils of anger and sadness pressing daily on my chest in the days before we take off. No one around us suspects a thing. Especially our girls. Because you see, they know what they are about to be missing.

They had been to Italy before, years earlier. Today they are sixteen and thirteen. During their only trip to Italy, they were ten and seven. If you sit them down and ask them about that trip to Italy they took years ago, they will smile and tell you they remember walking down a dirt road from a little mountain village toward some stables, plucking cherries right off the limbs of the trees. They will tell you about getting lost in the maze of alleys in Venice, trying to find our way back to the convent in Dorsoduro, where we had a barracks-like room the nuns rented for thirty-five dollars a night. (They locked their gates at 11 p.m., so we hurried. We didn't want Italian nuns mad at us.) They will tell you about gelato melting faster than they could scoop it in their mouths, about touching statues in the garden of the Guggenheim villa, about dodging *viperas* coiled on the paths that wound through the olive groves. They will remember they were happy.

And I'm not allowed to tell them why, if they were to come

on this trip, they'd never find that same brand of happiness, no matter how hard they looked. They can't imagine what they are missing, really. And for now that is a good thing.

II.
The Tail Gunner
from Chee-ka-goes

UNDICI.

I look back sometimes.
That first trip to Italy, the one we took with our daughters years and years ago, was close to perfect. I don't think I'm overdosing on nostalgia. I thought it was perfect the day we got home and that wonderful, warm feeling hasn't faded over the years. I normally hate traveling in groups of any size, but this group—our little family—got along. I don't remember any fighting or tantrums from children or adults. I don't recall any missed trains or delayed flights. As far as I remember, it never rained.

DODICI.

On that trip when our daughters were younger, we spent time in a tiny village in the northern part of Tuscany called Serra Pistoiese. This was my wife's village, or at least the place where her *people* lived. Since early in our marriage, I'd heard stories about how the Parenti family had ultimately made its way from tiny Serra to America. The village perches on the spine of a thin mountaintop, within sight of the more well-known and more frequented Italian Alps. Long and narrow, only a few hundred yards across at its widest point, Serra clings to slopes that drop off steeply at its eastern and western limits. During the winter, snows and winds batter Serra from November to March, and that's why the year-round population is small, mostly older men and women who possess neither the means nor the energy to leave. But in the summers, the population of Serra triples as Italians (including a number of families) escape the humidity and heat of Florence for the cooler heights of Serra Pistoiese.

The summer we were there with our girls, the village bustled. Vendors showed up in the mornings and set up impromptu markets in the widest part of the street, in the center of the village, selling everything from flip-flops to disposable razors. Some kid was always kicking a soccer ball against the side wall of the old convent. A couple of times a day an old woman with perfect posture and a constant frown dragged a homemade straw broom to the World War I monument near the single bus stop in the village and cleared the marble of leaves that had blown from the chestnut trees. It was her daily mission, her vigil. Under one of those large chestnuts outside the door of the village's only café, a loud card game ran all day long, players dipping in and out of hands, sliding their chairs to chase the shade.

Serra fascinated me, not because it photographed beautifully for postcards, but because it was the one place, the single dot on a map that pinpointed a person's honest-to-god beginning. This was where my wife was conceived—not literally, of course, but conceived in a narrative sense, in a storytelling way. Her story began here, in Serra, on this mountaintop. If that Parenti man had not impregnated his wife and put her on the boat in Naples with a few lire and a promise to join her soon, my wife would never have had a grandmother in Buffalo or a mother in D.C. Or by extension, a husband.

I know, I know—a clichéd sensation. Break out the red pen. Every mildly curious human can jump on ancestry.com or offer up some DNA or simply talk to old folks and get a sense of their origins. But this *felt* different. This wasn't a family tree sketched out on a sheet of notebook paper or a list penciled on the inside front cover of a family Bible. These were real people who had eyes the same shade as my wife's, as my daughters', people with noses with the exact slope of my wife's. This was a family tree that waved its arms, that offered me homemade limoncello, that told me stories first-hand.

I don't think I'd ever loved my wife more than during the days we were in Serra, when we'd brought our own little branch of the tree back to the widest part of its base, to the taproot. Through her, I had become something better, something bigger, and I'm positive that is the finest thing love can do.

TREDICI.

When we arrived in Serra back then, we soon discovered the collective English vocabulary in the village was maybe twenty words. We communicated with hand gestures and monosyllables for the most part. My wife's Italian wasn't bad, but I was continually lost and spent most of my time smiling and nodding at bursts of rapid-fire Italian I couldn't understand. We muddled through, until Antonluigi showed up.

Antonluigi drove up from Florence. Serra was his boyhood home, where he'd been raised by my wife's great-grandfather. And being raised as boy in Serra meant learning how to hunt *cinghiale*—the wild boar—and how to roast chestnuts properly in the winter, how to raise pigeons until they grew large enough to be an entrée and how to drive a horse-cart down the slope to the spring for water.

Antonluigi was a big-wig in Florence, an attorney and a city councilman. He promised to take us places most tour guides couldn't even conceive of: a backdoor tour of the Ufizzi Gallery where he would show us the secret panel in the secret room where Medici leaders lured their enemies, knifed them, then slid their bodies down a long chute into the Arno River; a restaurant with only four tables and food so orgasmic the reservation list was full for the next two years (yet he had a weekly slot); a marble carver who had actually laid a chisel on David. I am tempted to say he was, when we met, a dapper man, but dapper seems offensive when describing an Italian. Antonluigi wore suits custom cut to his slightly bowed lower back and his hair was always perfect. His shoes were made of leather that appeared as soft as tissue paper. But he was not a classically handsome man. His papery skin had grown tight and gray from too many years of unfiltered cigarettes, and he wore dentures that unfortunately did not fit as well as his suits. They continually popped loose as he talked, and he had to snap his jaws shut quickly to tongue them back into place.

I watched those dentures carefully the afternoon Antonluigi drove all of us deeper into the mountains to a tiny restaurant he loved. We sat there—me, my wife, my daughters—while Antonluigi told stories and chased his dentures around his mouth. My daughters were more interested in the food than the talking, twirling pasta on their forks and shoving the *cinghiale* ragout into hiding places on their plates because they couldn't imagine eating anything called wild boar.

Antonluigi was a natural storyteller. He knew how to introduce characters and when. He wasn't afraid to pause in places to let silence wash over us before he continued with a tale about getting horribly lost on a boar hunt with my wife's great-grandfather or about the ghost that walked the hallways of the old convent, reciting her rosary in Latin and clicking her beads together in time with her chanting. Once, toward the end of the lunch when the plates were cleared and the limoncello appeared, he turned to me and said, "You know this other story, yes? The big story. Important one. About gill foil?"

I looked at my wife for help with the translation. The word or words didn't sound Italian, but I couldn't place them. Gill foil. Gill-foil. He repeated the words as if their meaning would somehow crystallize if he chanted them enough. My wife shrugged and reached for the little pocket dictionary she kept in her purse. Antonluigi leaned forward and stopped her.

"No, no," he said, dentures ricocheting in his mouth. "It is a name." He pulled a pen from the breast pocket of his suit and grabbed the closest hand he saw—mine. Anyone else and I would have pulled away, but this was Italy...I was a stranger, this was a man on the Florence city council, this (I knew) was going to be a good story. He looked at my open hand for a couple of seconds like a palm reader, then carefully like a first grader who'd just learned penmanship, wrote a word across the lines: *Guilfoil*. "It is a name," he repeated.

After he put his pen away, Antonluigi sketched out the story of Guilfoil. I could tell this was a different type of narrative for him. He didn't smile as much when he spoke and his voice dropped to a reverent, respectful murmur.

"This," he said, "is the story everyone knows."

QUATTORDICI.

Guilfoil was a young man, barely military legal, from Chicago (or Chee-ka-goes, as Antonluigi pronounced it) who served as a tail gunner on a B-17 called the Rhomar II during the Second World War. On a bombing mission one October—"A very cold time for Serra," Antonluigi said—his plane was shot down high above the village. The villagers collected in the square, watching the dogfight and the subsequent parachutes in the valley to the east. All of the crew members except Guilfoil bailed out over the mountains. Guilfoil went down with his plane, into the thick forest on the hillside just below Serra.

"And we went there," Antonluigi said. "I was a little boy, but yes, I went too. We all did." According to Antonluigi, they found the plane quickly. The bomber had sheared the tops off a dozen massive chestnut trees when it crash-landed, but had not burst into flame. "There was smoke but no fire," he said. Guilfoil was dead inside. Nineteen years old. A long way from Chee-ka-goes.

But that wasn't his entire story. "The men take Guilfoil out of the plane. I have never seen a dead man. Or a dead boy, almost like me. And when he is out of the plane we have our own little war," he said.

The people from Serra gathered at the crash site decided they would load Guilfoil's body on a cart, take him back to Serra and bury him in their cemetery. They decided, almost without saying it, to give him a measure of respect, a proper burial in a foreign country. The villagers were no strangers to what happened in wartime, not unaccustomed to the deaths of young men too soon. This was something they could do. The soldiers that showed up a few minutes later had other plans for Guilfoil's body.

"The Nazis—and they were not the only ones, there were Fascists from the mountains who were the German..." and he paused, searching for a word. "*Como se diche?*" He pantomimed his yellow fingers moving the strings on a marionette.

"Puppets?" I said.

"Si, si, puppets. The Fascisti were the German puppets and they wanted to leave Guilfoil to the *cinghiale*. They said let the *cinghiale* have lunch with an American. They thought that was a funny joke. They had guns. We did not." Antonluigi stopped his story to take a sip of wine. Then, he began to glance around for the waiter. The pause was too long. The story hung in the air. I thought he had ended, but without a proper conclusion.

"What?" I said, immediately thinking I'd been rude.

"What do you mean, what?" Click, click inside his mouth.

"What happened to Guilfoil?"

A hybrid of hurt and disbelief rose in Antonluigi's eyes. I realized that he considered the Guilfoil story as legend, as a tale that everyone who stepped foot in Serra knew, or at least had been told. The fact that we'd never heard of the tail gunner from Chicago or the gathering of the villagers at the crash site and their plans to bury Guilfoil in their tiny cemetery had never crossed Antonluigi's mind.

"Impossible," he said. Then, "Really, you do not know what happened?"

My wife and I both shook our heads. My daughters did the same. The story of a dead, burning boy in an airplane had captured their interest too.

"Well," he said, standing and snapping his napkin from his lap, "we won. Serra beat the Fascisti. Guilfoil was buried in our cemetery. We stared at their guns until they melted." He laughed and called for the bill.

QUINDICI.

Later that evening, back in Serra, Antonluigi pulled me aside and asked me to wait while he looked for something. He dug in the back seat of his car, tossing aside a couple of wrinkled, white shirts and what seemed to be too many leather briefcases for one man, until he found what he was searching for—a large manila envelope. The only thing written on the outside was a date: *5 Ottobre 1943*.

"For you," he said. He saw I was confused. "This is about Guilfoil. I wrote to people, a few people, to find more about the story. This is not much, but it is more than I have told you."

I put my hands out to my sides, as if to say I didn't understand. He continued. "Your wife tells me you are the *autore*." He translated for me. "Author, a writer. You should write about Guilfoil."

Several times a year, people bring me their stories, asking me to write them down. The conversations usually begin: *I'm not a writer, but lord do I have a story somebody should put on paper. I'll give it to you.* And like a literary Santa Claus, they open their present to me.

I usually tell these people I have enough stories of my own and not enough time to co-op someone else's. But Antonluigi was different. He wasn't looking for someone to transcribe his oral history of Guilfoil and the crash in the woods. There was something else. I saw a fear lurking into his eyes. The people who were alive when Guilfoil went down in the woods were dying off. And Guilfoil's story, he was afraid, would die with them. Antonluigi wanted Guilfoil to survive, to remain the best story you could hear about Serra, not just a rumor of something that happened to a stranger during a war nobody talked about anymore. He was determined to keep Guilfoil alive, as determined as those people were in 1943 to bury him in the little cemetery on the road out of town.

But I didn't want to be Guilfoil's keeper. I didn't care about him or his plane or his cemetery plot. And I didn't write about fighter pilots or Italians or war. I wondered how to decline and not offend.

Antonluigi noticed my hesitation. "Just look," he said, tapping the envelope in my hands. "Just a look. Take it home with you. Keep it. I have my copy. This is yours. You will want it someday." He turned to walk back into the house where we were having dinner. I tucked the envelope under my arm. On the other side of the cobblestone street, an older man hollered to Antonluigi in Italian.

"*Buona sera*," Antonluigi called back, then clapped me on the shoulder. He yelled across the street again. "*Autore, eh? Guilfoil!*" And when he said that name, the man across the street turned his hand palm-down and pantomimed an airplane gliding in front of him, a simple homage to Guilfoil and to a story so many seemed to know.

SEDICI.

Paolo Parenti is my wife's distant cousin. Somehow. I can never keep up when people recite their lineages, but Paolo, it seems, is the son of a great-great-aunt, which would make him a fourth or fifth cousin. Or something like that. If you stood my wife and Paolo side by side, you might call them brother and sister, rather than vague cousins. They possess the same slope on the bridges of their noses, and their nostrils flare the same way when they laugh too hard. I watched Paolo roll his eyes while his wife told a story about him, and I knew I'd seen that exasperated expression before. My wife and her Italian cousin even waved their hands in similar directions when they were excited, as if they'd received semaphore lessons from the same flag instructor.

Physically, the similarities stopped there. While my ex-dancer wife floated when she walked and trusted her feet implicitly to carry her over the mine field of cobblestones in Serra's streets, Paolo picked his way along, hunched a little to guard his chronically bad back. When I asked him what was wrong with his back (and Antonluigi translated my question) Paolo pointed at the basketball-sized pot belly fighting with his belt buckle and gave me an expression that said, *Hey, if you had to carry this around on the front, wouldn't your back hurt, too?*

The way he talked, Paolo wasn't a typical Italian. His hands, while they fluttered and wind milled on occasions, stayed relatively calm compared to other Serra residents. When he spoke, he murmured quietly and we all leaned in to try and pick up a word or two. He was a mellow Italian, which is a top-shelf oxymoron. But Paolo's wife more than made up for his calmness.

Renza was a constant tornado of sound and motion, capped by her head of flaming red hair, a store-bought shade not found naturally. Whatever Renza had to say, she announced like an Italian carnival barker, her hands karate-chopping the air as though she was in battle with it. Renza would enter the room and accost Paolo with a machine-gun burst of loud Italian and symphony-conductor gesticulations, and I would think, My god, he's killed someone and she's found the body in the basement, only to discover she wanted to know what time she should plan dinner.

But Renza loved my daughters in the way only Italians worship children. She doted over them as if they were visiting dignitaries, giving them first choices of everything: food, seats, small gifts from the street vendors. She was particularly interested in E—our tiny one—because, I guess, of her size. Perhaps Renza had never seen a miniature human, at least one who could talk and laugh at the pidgin English Renza threw out in her attempts to infiltrate conversations. I think she was fascinated by the fact that nature or God or whomever had halted a little girl in mid-growth and was attempting to keep her there. Renza considered it amazing that my oldest daughter might never get old because she would never get tall, and for an Italian that was akin to a miracle: a child who remained a child forever.

Her child—Renza and Paolo's daughter—was a balanced blend of her father's mildness and her mother's manic energy. In her early twenties, Silvia was jaded in the best possible way. That is, she found her mother amusing and wasn't the least bit embarrassed by Renza's whirling dervish mannerisms. And while she poked fun at her father's nearly silent presence, she clearly adored him in that way only a daughter can care for a father. Silvia could fire an outburst reminiscent of her mother and moments later be a quiet, smiling listener at the dinner table. Her appearance also owed something to both parents. She had the Parenti nose beneath a burst of flaming, fake-red hair. Most usefully for us, she spoke a smattering of English, so she could serve as

Scott Gould

translator when Antonluigi returned to Florence in the late afternoons.

Their house had been a hotel in a former life, and it loomed over the middle of town. Five stories high, the staircase disappeared into long hallways where some of the doors still had room numbers tacked to them. It was way too much house for Paolo's family (which at that time also included his elderly in-laws, Renza's parents Vivetta and Remo), but Italian families tended to expand through the years, rather than shrink.

Paolo was the unofficial mayor of Serra. When folks called to him from the card game in front of the café or from a window in the old convent, I detected an air of respect in their words. And because we were eating dinner with Paolo, because we were hiking down to his acre-and-a-half garden, because we were sipping wine at his table, we were—by mere association and the accident of genealogy—very important people for a few days. We were the distant relatives from America. For some reason, they all thought we knew about Guilfoil.

It was as if Antonluigi had announced to everyone in Serra that I had been bequeathed his story, and it was now okay to ask *me* for details. A man with maybe six teeth in his head wearing a crisp white shirt walked up to me one evening and said, in very rehearsed, toneless English: "And how is the Guilfoil family doing in Chicago, United States?"

I realized the time warp I had entered. For the people of Serra, Guilfoil was still alive, or at least his story was. Guilfoil was the one thing they possessed that no one else had. Whatever pride the tiny little village maintained, it was embodied in a nineteen-year old fly boy from Chicago who happened to crash and die in their backyard. Each time someone told the story, it was October, 1943 all over again, the month Serra puffed out its chest and stared down a little slice of the Third Reich.

Antonluigi wanted me to help save Guilfoil, help save a guy who'd been dead for decades.

46

DICIASSETTE.

One night, Paolo tugged me into rooms in his ex-hotel's inner sanctums. I saw the space where he displayed the taxidermied heads of deer and wild boar he and Remo hunted when they were both younger and possessed the energy to stalk animals up and down the hills below the village. He took me to the top floor of the hotel, where I could see, on the horizon far to the north, the summer snow still on several peaks of the Italian Alps. He was treating me differently, and this was a relief. I had begun to feel like somewhat of an outsider around the dinner table. I was the only person sitting there who wasn't related to the others. In my daughters—with their brown eyes and olive skin—I could see their mother. And in their mother, I could see Paolo. I saw the Parenti features peeking out at me. They were connected, each of them. (Sure, Renza may have been genetically out of the mix on the Parenti side, but she was a moving target. She was never still enough to examine. And, perhaps not so oddly, she looked remarkably like Paolo.)

I may have felt like an outsider, but Paolo did his best to bring me into his little fold. One evening, after dinner, he disappeared into the bowels of the ex-hotel and returned with dusty bottles of homemade limoncello and basilica, a basil liqueur. Renza dealt out tiny café glasses. My wife huddled with Silvia in the next room, practicing her Italian. Our daughters were asleep on the long sofa in the front room, near the door, worn out from the day. Paolo walked outside into the dark and in a matter of half a minute, returned with three men, a trio I'd seen anchored most afternoons to a bench outside the café.

Paolo directed me to a seat at the small dining room table. The other men grabbed chairs like they had been here before and possessed assigned seats. After Paolo poured us each a sampling of the limoncello, he sat and slapped the table with his palms, perhaps the most demonstrative gesture I'd ever seen from him. I thought maybe we were starting a card game.

"*Cinghiale!*" Paolo said a little loudly. Renza rolled her eyes in the background.

Then Paolo fired some Italian at his friends. They rubbed their hands together. Paolo was probably the youngest of the group. All weathered men, their toothy smiles exploded when Paolo held up a small pepper shaker.

"*Cinghiale,*" he repeated, nodding to the pepper. He placed it in the center of the table. One of the men, whose name I think was Raymond or Raymon, grabbed the pepper shaker and ran it around the surface of the table in crazy circles, like he was pushing a toy Hot Wheels car.

"Hunting *cinghiale,*" Raymon said, the English word *hunting* leaping out of his mouth and scaring me.

For the next twenty minutes, the men demonstrated how they stalked wild boar, using salt and pepper shakers and small bottles of oil and hot peppers and the corks from limoncello bottles as stand-ins for hunters and the hunted. With condiments, they demonstrated how some men would drive the *cinghiale* while the others flanked the animal's movements. They surrounded the pepper shakers with the other bottles. And finally Paolo flicked the pepper shaker to its side with his finger, knocking it over. "Boom," he said, and the men gave out a small, quiet cheer.

It was summertime. *Cinghiale* season occurs during the cold months, but they'd managed to take me on a hunt with them. Paolo pulled me into his circle. I'd like to think it was because he liked me and found me interesting, but probably, he was motivated by the fact I was the only male visitor in his house. Like me, he spent his time surrounded by females. Me? I was a new man under his roof, a potential hunting companion, even if we only surrounded a pepper shaker.

That final night, we carried our sleeping daughters to the

rental station wagon and said our goodbyes in the street outside Paolo's house. The card game had long closed down. Someone still walked in the café, sweeping the floor. We had been around each other long enough to hug, days before having passed that invisible boundary of intimacy.

When I broke away from Renza, she shook her finger at me and rattled off a quick Italian phrase. She seemed frustrated she couldn't find the English she needed. She glanced toward her daughter and Silvia translated. "She says you will come back again," and I couldn't tell if it was a question or a command.

DICIOTTO.

I never saw Antonluigi again. We received word of his passing long after the fact, and even when I heard he was gone, I didn't feel moved to dive into Guilfoil's life and take up his story. I had looked inside the envelope once, right when I returned home. It was interesting, but not interesting enough. Mostly official reports of the crash. A single photo of the Rhomar II crew. Too many other things tugged at my time. I had plenty of excuses to avoid Guilfoil. Daughters were growing up, or in E's case, being lengthened by an intricate arrangement of wires and metal rings and camshafts. I was in the midst of an advertising job that daily nibbled away tiny sections of my soul. My wife was happy half the time and spent the other half worrying about why she wasn't happy *all* the time. I slid the envelope under some shoe boxes on the shelf in my closet and left it there and forgot about Antonluigi and Guilfoil and the sounds things make when they crash down.

III.
Dead Man Signs

19.

I learn the meaning of lag time. There are three weeks before the two of us leave for Italy, and we know something the rest of the world doesn't. We sit at the kitchen table for dinner, and our daughters do their comedy act, their re-creation of the day, complete with impersonations and punch lines, and we all giggle with our mouths full, but two of us know secrets. She doesn't look at me when she laughs.

Still in the same bed, the same old bed, which is now odd and uncomfortable. This lying on eggshells. I don't know how to act, but I imagine this is how someone with a terminal illness might feel. What she doesn't realize is that I am gathering strength, making plans, lining up my proverbial ducks into a row for the trip, the last trip. You see, she thinks that when she hustles off to Mass on Sunday mornings, I am in the little room off the hallway, working on that screenplay I've been talking about for years. But instead of scene descriptions and dialog, I'm writing sentences and phrases again and again. *You will figure this out. You will hit the shot. Watch the clock. Watch the clock.* Like Nicholson in *The Shining*, going crazy quietly on my own, writing nonsense after nonsense after nonsense.

20.

I'm not that guy, the one who remembers every quarter of every game he played in high school, as if something that transpired at age seventeen represents the pinnacle of a life's achievement. But one Sunday morning while I sit there filling up a legal pad page with mantras, I recall the end of one particular basketball game in high school.

We were playing a team from Brookland-Cayce, a city school. The bigger schools liked to pad their schedules with us. We were still country then, not even suburbia. City always expects to beat country. I'm sure the gym was hot and smelled like warm popcorn. The cold just outside the doors leaked into the lobby, and the squeak of sneakers cut through all the other sounds. We trailed by a couple of points with, I think, three or four seconds left on the clock, not much time to tie things up. I wandered around, out near the half court line, like I was lost, a couple of their players tailing me every time I changed direction. One of our guys lobbed the ball toward half court, toward me. The chances of catching the ball, squaring up and making something from forty-five feet were too slim to consider. As the ball arched toward us, I remember one of the Brookland-Cayce guys crowding me a little closer than I expected. Then, he nudged me, probably by accident. Not much. Just enough to be noticeable. So I flopped.

I threw my hands out and smacked the floor like a sniper had nailed me from the back row of the bleachers. The ball sailed over my head. The referee caught my flop in his peripheral vision and blew his whistle. I got two free

Scott Gould

throws, made them both, and we tied the game. We won it
in overtime. But that's not important. What's important is I
learned the value of a decent fake.

I decide to flop in Italy. I won't get mad. I will not get frustrated. I will fake it all. She thinks I will crumble or grovel
(or suffer some sort of psychotic break among the sunflower
fields in Tuscany). I am banking on the fact that she doesn't
know how to recognize a flop in the fourth quarter. It is good
I remember that game.

With that memory buzzing in my head, I begin to write
on my pad, over and over: *Fake everything. Fake everything.*

21

So we let the day arrive. To the world outside of our secret, nothing appears out of place. We are just two people going through the typical stresses of preparing for a long trip. We double-check flight schedules, calculate parking rates at the airport. She writes list after list. Our daughters tease us about how much we pack. E holds up her mother's bathing suit and groans about how small it is. M wonders why I'm even taking long pants. They laugh because they are old enough to make fun of adults now. My wife and I don't make eye contact. I never realized how little you could actually look at someone you lived with, if you really tried. But we laugh too, separately, in different rooms. We can't share that. The only thing we can share is that we don't tell anyone. The secret. The weight. The looming thing.

We exchange some money ahead of time, just enough to get us going when we arrive in Italy. We make photocopies of our passports and slide the pages into our suitcases because she read somewhere this is an important thing to do. We stock up on film and Ibuprofen and miniature versions of necessary things: deodorant and shampoo and mouthwash. We are normal and painfully abnormal at the same time.

I lie there at night with her (because sleeping anywhere else would arouse suspicion, would bring the looming thing to light) and stare at the ceiling fan paddling the air in the dark and imagine. Imagine how I'm going to win, how I'm going to save this. I plan the fake. I write scenarios in my head, because that's what I've done for years: make up stories that turn out the way I want them to. I write silent dialog in my head. She has no trouble sleeping. She thinks she can see the future out there, is convinced she can see how this thing, this trip, will turn out. She doesn't know that right next to her, I'm doing revisions, rewriting all of her drafts about the days ahead.

E and M grow crankier as the day grows closer. They are still not comfortable with the fact that we'll be in Serra, with Paolo and Renza and Silvia, and they'll be stuck in South Carolina, wiping the humidity off their faces and swatting mosquitoes.

It is the last Sunday before we leave. The girls are sleeping in. I sit in the oddly shaped chair she bought at some auction. It's my writing chair. The cushions are big enough and comfortable enough, I can sit and write for hours. She is on her way to Mass, dashing out quickly, to pray or meditate or ask forgiveness. She has been going to Mass regularly lately, and it scares me some. She is recruiting God for her team. I wonder if I can still pull the game out in the fourth quarter with God on her side. The yellow pad balances on my knee.

Before she leaves, she sticks her head in the room, which is strange these days. Since announcing her big plans in the kitchen days and days ago, she no longer lets me in on the little ones. These days, she doesn't say she is going for a run or to the store or to Mass. She just leaves, as if she is rehearsing for her final exit. But this morning, she stands near the doorway, peering in. She is dressed a little casually for church, even if it is the early service.

"Hey," she says by way of an intro. It sounds almost friendly, which makes me afraid to answer. "I just need to say something," she continues. I still don't answer. I don't want to make it too easy for her. She lets the silence linger too long. "I just want to say that this isn't a test, you know. This trip, I mean. It isn't like I'm giving you a test you can pass or fail."

She waits for a second to see if I answer, then turns to go when I say nothing. I've become good at being quiet when I have nothing to say. I hear her car start in the garage, and I begin writing on the pad: *But it really is a test. But it really is a test. But it really is a test...* over and over in perfect, straight lines.

I wonder what else about this trip won't be the truth.

VENTIDUE.

I had forgotten how the summer heat in the valley around Florence seems to funnel maniacally into Galileo Airport. On the morning we land, I can tell from the window of the plane, it's scalding outside. The men and women sweat through their shirts as they drive baggage carts and direct planes to their gates. The heat doesn't simply shimmer on the tarmac—it billows in waves from the cement, even though it's only mid-morning.

The customs area is un-air-conditioned and (surprisingly) untended. Our bags lie in haphazard piles against a far wall and we grab what belongs to us. Heat breeds anger, especially among travelers who have flown through the night, and I'm already girding myself for the inevitable encounter with the customs agent, who no doubt will be sleepy and hot and sweaty and primed to exercise his tiny dose of power. But there are no agents in sight, no booths, no maze-like chutes to herd us through the process. There is, however, a door with a sign that reads *Exit to Airport*. Across from that sign is another exit door, and I decide to try that one. It leads directly into the steaming main parking lot of the Galileo Airport. We haul our bags behind us. We have entered the country without being stamped, without being questioned. I think: It's like I'm not even fucking here. And even in the swelter that smells like diesel and tar, the irony feels a little chilly. Like I'm not even here.

VENTITRÉ.

Picking up a rental car in Italy is a very un-American experience. No neat counters inside the airport, no neck-tied agents with thousand-watt smiles blaring above their uniforms. At the Galileo Airport, the car rental companies occupy small trailers on the perimeter of a huge parking lot. The trailers, which crackle metallically in the heat, have space for two, maybe three agents and a couple of customers, at most. There are no uniforms to identify the employees. If someone is hot and sweaty and pulling a suitcase, that's the customer. If someone is hot and sweaty and screaming in Italian and tossing keys, he is the rental company employee. If you possess what seems to be official paperwork, pages that come from a computer printer perhaps, you will get a car. The employee simply gestures with his hand or his chin toward a general area of the parking lot, and off you trek, tugging your bags through the gooey asphalt.

Our car is supposed to be a diesel VW. I find a little gaggle of Volkswagens, all of them unlocked, and I try a half dozen of them before I find one that lets my key fire the engine. The tires seem inflated. The AC works. I'm fairly sure I can handle the gearbox. I feel better immediately. But then I remember I'm walking on eggshells. I load her bag for her. I open her door. I ask her if she would like to drive. She rolls her eyes, the Parenti roll.

The exit from the Galileo Airport slingshots you into the traffic zooming in and out of Florence, which means you are thrust suddenly among crazy, possibly homicidal people with steering wheels in their hands and a ton and a half of

Scott Gould

metal under their asses. I know the only way to drive with
the Italians is to drive *like* the Italians, adopt their brand
of mobile insanity. I downshift on the ramp and dive into
the flow of cars. I glance at her, and she has her eyes closed,
the AC vents blowing her hair a little. We're here and nobody
officially checked us in. We can be who we need to be, who we
want to be. I take that as an omen, a positive one, as I drive
toward the mountains. I haven't even looked at a map yet.

VENTIQUATTRO.

I will say this: I try from the very start to be perfect. I know. Bad idea. But it's all I got.

Be perfect and make no mistakes. That is how you win basketball games in the final thirty seconds. It should work in Italy. I don't think anything will be lost in the translation. Here's what I imagine: She will look over at me one day, maybe in a restaurant in Lucca, just as the sun dips behind the wall that surrounds the city, and she will think, This man is perfect. I can't possibly run away from perfection.

I'm an idiot. I know this. But I try anyway. (If you prefer, call this courage. Or desperation.) So in the mornings, I make sure to get up early, before her, and make coffee in one of those odd, faceted Italian coffee pots. Making her coffee in the mornings isn't new. I've been doing it for years, even though I hate hot drinks, especially coffee. I enjoy the whole process. I like the smell. I don't like drinking it. Making her coffee in Italy, even when she's said she's leaving me—this seems like a minute, wonderful thing to do. It smacks of perfection.

I spend hours bird-dogging her through tiny shops in tiny villages, where she buys items that suddenly seem necessary to her, like squares of thin handmade wrapping paper or dried herbs tied into bundles with yarn. I stand in these shops, shifting my weight back and forth to give my aching knee a break. (I am eating Ibuprofen like popcorn. But I haven't so much as grimaced, because a grimace is an imperfection. You don't fucking grimace at the end of the game.

You don't let the other team know how you feel.) I try to look *passionate* about herbs. "That's perfect," I say when she examines a particular square of paper.

For a half day, I follow her around a town in the valley below Serra called Montecatini Terme, looking for olive oil soap, and I follow, carrying packages, swallowing the pain firing out of my left knee. She wants to bring soap to friends back home, our friends, people who will probably have to choose sides if I can't be perfect and pull this out.

She carries a list in her purse, names of all the people she has to buy some sort of Italian knick-knack for, small things that won't take up much room. I watch her mark off the names, and it occurs to me that these people will assume *she* bought these presents and I had nothing to do with it. I think: She is buying friends like someone purchases futures on the stock market. She is planning for the aftermath, for after the crash.

She's thinking ahead, but that shouldn't surprise me. She's plotted this in her head, months and months ahead of me. I'm not sure she realizes I'm watching when she pays for a couple of gifts and slides them quickly into a bag. I can't tell what they are. Maybe one was a wallet. She doesn't mark off a name this time. The listless gifts could be for me; she'll break them out later, right?

One afternoon, we are in the outdoor market in Florence, street after street of vendors selling food and clothes and junk. I follow my wife as she weaves through the stalls. I nod and smile while she fingers the slick material on a blouse. "The girls would love these," she says, patting some leather handbags, knock-offs of a more expensive Italian brand. "Love them," I repeat as brightly as I can. The mention of our girls hits deep in my stomach and almost bends me over, makes me forget about the knee.

It is hot in the market that morning and the air isn't moving. She suddenly stops and turns to me, and I think this could be a turning point. *(Time is running down! Gould has the ball. He checks the clock...)* She leans up to me, cupping my face—an actual touch.

It's working, I think. My plan is working. I've been perfect.

I've smiled when I didn't want to, acted interested when all I wanted was a tall, cold Peroni and a handful of Ibuprofen.

She whispers, as if she doesn't want anyone in the Florence flea market to hear. "Stop it. Please. You can't make this better, no matter how hard you try."

And just like that, she throws a grenade in my plan. She's known all along what was going on. I'm struck dumb, and I stand there looking at her, holding her bags, still shifting my weight back and forth on the noisy Italian eggshells beneath my feet.

VENTICINQUE.

The villa we share with our friends is a confusion of space. Just off the kitchen, an ancient pergola groans under the weight of its vines. Dark, maze-like hallways lead to rooms which open to more rooms which open to more hallways. The oversized windows in the bedrooms are never closed, and a constant breeze billows the floor-length curtains, giving the illusion of mainsails filling. There are dozens of places to get lost.

Outside the villa sits a bocce court of dusty crushed stone, and beyond the court, a narrow road leads to a decent-sized village. In the village, a woman in the cheese store tells me about the men's names on the street signs. She says the signs memorialize locals—all men—that have been killed by the Mafia. I find myself taking pictures of their names, thinking I might have something in common with them. I shoot an entire roll of black-and-white film. Nothing but photos of dead names on street signs.

One afternoon, the villa echoes from emptiness. Our friends have walked into the village to buy things for dinner—cheese and pasta and wine. I don't know where she is because I'm trying to avoid keeping close tabs on her. I want her to think I'm granting her that space she talked about. I wander inside the villa and notice the silence.

A breeze funnels through the narrow halls. I make my way to the bathroom adjacent to the room we were assigned. On the other side of the bathroom door, I hear her enter our bedroom. I clear my throat to let her know I am close by. I am a little disappointed because I want to take a nap. I don't want another discussion. I don't want another person in the same room. I hear the bed springs jangle, followed by the slide of sheets on skin. I'll have to nap somewhere else. She beat me to it.

Then she issues The First Invitation. Through the closed door, I hear the words, and it's a new language she must be studying. Not Italian. Another language. Translation? She invites me to bed.

But there is nothing romantic about The First Invitation. Just a single, raw line that sounds stolen from a blue movie scene, telling me precisely what she wants. It's her voice. I recognize that, but it takes me by surprise, and my answer is more of a stall tactic than anything else. "What?" I say.

So she repeats herself and The First Invitation is as empty as the villa. It has nothing to do with napping. And if I was confused before I walked into the bathroom, I'm utterly addled now. (Can you blame me? Think about it: the woman who is planning her escape, who wants her space, now wants me.) But it isn't her; it can't be. I mean, it's her voice, but the words are lifted from a new vocabulary. After seventeen years, I know the things my wife says and I know how she says them. This has to be some type of crazy ventriloquist act.

I finish using the bathroom and look down. Nothing happening there. I am paralyzed head to toe—and every body part in between. I'm not sure if I'm supposed to obey or flee down the hall. I had not anticipated this scenario. (In the fourth quarter, when you're behind and playing catch-up, surprises like this can cost you the game.) I have to be smart, and when I'm in trouble, my default reaction is to try and be funny. Maybe I'll ask her if I need to RSVP that invitation. Something light like that. If I can make her laugh, perhaps some of the tension I'm suddenly feeling in the bathroom will leak through the open window and into the field beyond the bocce court.

I walk into the bedroom, leading with my failure. She looks me up and down. She is still hunting for that passion, and I'm still looking for answers, and those two searches will not mesh this afternoon in the confusing space of the villa. I end up napping in an empty room down the hall. *But it really is a test.*

VENTISEI.

There is The Second Invitation, at the pool. The pool shimmers in the heat at the end of a short, broken path that winds from the villa. No trees surround it, so the water catches sun the entire day. On one side, the pool deck drops down toward the yellow hay fields below the villa, and on the other, the narrow, paved road to the village runs not more than fifty feet from the water. Because it is so unprotected and in the open, it feels like a public pool. All of us—she, I and our friends—spend mornings and afternoons by the water, when we aren't walking into the village or catching a train for a daytrip to Florence or Lucca.

One morning just as the sun begins to climb above the trees, she suggests we go for a swim. (This is not The Second Invitation. Call it The Pre-Invitation.) This is a couple of days after the bedroom/bathroom encounter, which we never discuss, because we don't talk if we don't have to. I convince myself this is why she wants to go to the pool, that maybe she has come to the conclusion we should discuss the constant weirdness filling up the villa. I'm sure our friends have noticed that the two of us seem like high school kids on a bad first date.

When we reach the pool, she spreads a long towel on the cement near the edge of the deck, where it slopes down to the fields. Without looking, I can tell hay is being cut—the sharp, sour smell is thick in the air and I hear the distant rattle of tractors. She reaches behind to undo the clasp on her bathing suit top. She issues The Second Invitation in her new language, with a specific location in mind: "Right here," she says.

I know how I am supposed to act, and it would be easy if I knew the person sitting on the towel. But a stranger has asked something of me. All I see are bad outcomes. What will happen if our friends return? What if the men on the tractors glance up the hill? What about cars driving by? Villagers in their beat-up Renaults might pump their squeaky breaks and watch us wrestle each other on the cement. She told me I couldn't save things, but maybe this is her way of giving me another shot. (So to speak.) Then again, she'd said to stop trying. What is this, if not a try at something? I make a joke about a pair of full moons in broad daylight. Then I mention people might see us. I can't think of anything else to say, so I stop. I hesitate too long. I have the ball at the end of the game and I freeze. She nods and smiles as if she's won a prize. "See," she says, folding her arms back into the straps of her bathing suit. "It's the passion again. You have none. I need passion daily. You don't understand a damn thing about passion. You never listen."

She shakes her head and laughs at me and walks back to the villa, leaving me standing on the hot cement, breathing in the smell of new-cut hay. But she is wrong. I listen. I hear everything, even the new language she suddenly speaks.

Legal pad pages swim in front of my eyes, lines and lines of yellow sentences: *But it really is a test. But it really is a test*, and I think I might actually be going insane.

VENTISETTE.

I walk back into town and take more pictures of street signs
decorated with dead men.

Ventotto.

We plan a day trip to Serra, to see her family, and she invites our friends to come along. When she describes Serra to them, the village takes on a magical, storybook feel. She waves her hands and tells them about the way the village balances on the mountainside, about the drunken switchbacks on the road leading up the mountain, about the tiny cobblestone streets that snake in and out of the buildings. I watch the sudden desire to experience a strange place flood their faces. They look at me for confirmation, and I nod like a ventriloquist's dummy. I am dreading this. I'm scared Serra will be the place where the entire trip to Italy implodes on itself, that I will suffer a breakdown, right there on the uneven cobblestones in front of Paolo's hotel/house.

VENTINOVE.

I have forgotten the time warp that surrounds Serra until we pull into the village one hot mid-afternoon. The last time I had been there was years ago, with E and M in tow, when Antonluigi was our guide. Since then, nothing has changed in Serra. The same perpetual card game unfolds under the chestnut tree, in front of the café. Paolo's house still looms over all of the proceedings, sentinel-like. There is a sad, pithy irony in knowing that Serra is the same as it has always been, while in my world, everything is dramatically altered.

Renza greets us at the door. Her hair is still a shade of flame-red. Paolo actually looks younger, like he has peeled back some years. He is standing straighter and has lost some of the weight below his belt buckle. He has a younger posture these days. I tell him, in broken Italian, that his back must be feeling better, and he performs a little stretch from side to side to show me how pain free he is. He is smiling; in fact, they all are grinning widely, happy to see us, happy to have the Americans back in town.

My wife is a minor celebrity when she visits, an honorary villager, a prodigal. She seems to maintain some sort of ownership within the village. Or perhaps it's the other way around, perhaps the people of Serra maintain some sort of ownership of her. When we step out of the car, eyes are everywhere, spying on our arrival. Heads appear in window frames, peek around corners, everyone looking at her. They no doubt notice what I've noticed: how much she and Paolo favor each other, how even the web of laugh lines at their eyes spread in the same patterns. She is a native, removed only by time and space, not by blood. The rest of us? We are tag-alongs, the entourage. We are granted a small measure of respect, but their real love is reserved for her, because of who she is. And who she is, is the woman who lives in America, the confident, blonde, smiling American, who still comes back to visit the little ancestral village on the hill.

Inside Paolo's house, we sit where space allows—around the tiny dining room table or on the couch or in the straight-backed chairs scattered throughout the big room. Nothing has changed inside Paolo's house. The same photographs line the wall and prop on the tables. I let my gaze wander and notice the one new picture, a framed eight-by-ten of my family during our last trip, taken near the barn below the village where the girls ate cherries off the branches. I feel my eyes begin to well up and I get ready to excuse myself to the bathroom when I sense her stare locked on me.

Her look tells me I need to keep my shit together, that this would be the most damaging place to create a scene. If the real story of us, that looming thing, were to breech the light of day here, in Serra, it would embarrass her in the worst way possible. With the expression she fires across the room at me, she isn't begging me *not* to have the breakdown I've been dreading, rather she's daring me to try.

Nobody sees the looks that cross between us. Our friends are enamored with Paolo and his family. They treat this like a Disney attraction, and they are acting like kids. They ask dozens of questions. They ooh and ahh when Paolo breaks out the limoncello, then laugh when Renza chides him for drinking so early in the day. He says nothing, just shrugs his shoulders and continues to fill the small café glasses when they grow empty.

Silvia is not around; she is somewhere down the mountain with friends. "She'll join us later," Renza says. Vivetta walks down the stairs and her appearance startles me. She is ghost-like, so thin and light. She doesn't appear to make contact with the floor as she shuffles along. She forces a smile at us. Paolo leans toward my ear and tells me in economical English that Remo died a half year ago, and

Scott Gould

Vivetta has spent the better part of the last few months in
her room, eating little and talking less. I feel bad I didn't
notice his absence the minute we arrived, and I realize that
I am not taking in the world like I should, not being obser-
vant. My head is filled up with too much of myself and my
problems. Vivetta sits in the chair that is always reserved
for her, and we continue our staccato conversations, relying
more on hand gestures than on language. We've been asked
to stay for dinner—that much I pick up from scattering of
Italian and English. Renza wants to know about our girls,
so I hold my hands out in front of me to show their respec-
tive heights. E is still small, and when I hold my hand low
in front of me, Renza smiles. I remember that E is a favorite
of hers. Her lack of height makes her unique, and in Renza's
world, the unique are appreciated.

TRENTA.

That evening, we sit around the old, large table in Paolo's dining room and eat like villagers. Renza has dusted zucchini flowers with what looks like cornmeal and fried them in olive oil until the outside crisps up. She uses the same oil for pigeon breasts and rabbit pieces. She dices zucchini and tomatoes into a sauce and ladles it over pasta. The basket of bread is in constant motion around the table except when Vivetta leaves to refill it. She is in charge of the bread. And she is happier. I see a smile creep into her cheeks as she listens to the broken bits of conversation and the mistakes in translations.

I can't take my eyes off the fixtures on the table, the salt and pepper shakers and the tiny jar of hot peppers in oil and the jar of olives. Without thinking, I start to arrange them in front of me, the same way Paolo did when he explained the *cinghiale* hunt years before. Paolo sees me fiddling with the condiments, and smiles, remembering that night, too, I hope.

I flick the pepper over. "Boom," I say, and he laughs, perhaps too loudly, and no one else at the table is in on our joke. They stop their conversations and look over at us, but I just throw up my hands and shake my head. "It would be a long, boring story," I tell them. "Sorry."

She continues to stare at me, wondering if I've done it, wondering if I've somehow told Paolo everything and he's laughing at her. She suspects me of something. I feel it in her glare. And then it hits me: she suspects me of having a moment of happiness in this room. That would violate a law, some sort of code of conduct she has developed for this looming thing, a set of rules I haven't been allowed to see. But now, I know. For all of this to work, for her to be able to make an exit to this other life she is molding, I have to be miserable. I *have* to be devastated, and the fact that I laughed (and even worse, made somebody else laugh) when I ticked over a pepper shaker suggests I might be growing comfortable with my impending losses. I think this is the stupidest idea I've ever heard of, and it makes me hate her more than I imagined I ever could. There, with the remnants of Renza's dinner littering the table, I realize I am married to the most selfish person I've ever met. And I match her, glare for glare across the table, until she breaks her gaze and turns to our friends. I count this as a tiny win.

That night, on the way down the mountain, we pack into the van one of our friends rented. She and I don't sit together; it is easy enough to avoid each other when we randomly pile into the back seats. We creep through the switchbacks slowly because we are unfamiliar with the curves and full of Paolo's limoncello. When the van grows too silent, I explain Paolo's reaction to the pepper shaker. I tell them the strategy of boar hunting, but I don't stop there. I recite the short version of the Guilfoil story, about the boy who crashed in Serra and was rescued by the village, even after his death.

Everyone—except her—agrees Guilfoil's is a story I should write down. I don't recall her saying a word the entire trip back to the villa.

TRENTUNO.

The dinner in Serra and the return down the mountain—this is my only period of clarity, the only time I feel I understand something important. I caught a glimpse of who she is—or has become—and that vision gives me a sense that I might actually heal over one day, form some scar tissue. (Now I know I can still talk! Still tell stories! All while knowing the woman across the table from me is leaving in a matter of weeks. I feel my backbone straighten for a few seconds.) But it doesn't last.

The next morning, I want so much to remain the guy who can glare right back at her, match her stare-for-stare, but in that new daylight, I cannot bring myself to look her dead in the eye. I am still trying to save things, which means I can't fight back, can't be too aggressive. At least I think that's what it means. I am still trying to be the ballplayer looking for an edge, an angle. I don't want to lose as the clock runs out, because losing means saying goodbye to her, means breaking our daughters' hearts, means being alone. So I keep my eyes down and toe a line I've somehow drawn in the sand without really knowing it.

Just before dark, I dig a phone card out of my suitcase, one that still has some minutes to burn. I thought the day had begun to cool down, but I'm sweating by the time I reach the payphone at the café. We're not using our cell phones in Italy. The international plan is too expensive. At least I'm not using mine; I'm not sure about her. We're quickly coming to the point where we make no decisions in tandem, even something as trivial as whether or not to turn on a cell phone.

On the way to the payphone, I realize I've forgotten to swallow some Ibuprofen, and when the bones in my knee begin to grind against each other, the pain flies up my spine and hammers the back of my neck. I punch in the numbers of my own phone, at my own house, and it strikes me that I don't know how much longer I'll be living there. I mean, she says she is leaving, but I'm not sure how literal she is being. She is planning to leave a lot of things; maybe the house isn't one of them.

Who is moving where? I wonder. We haven't talked about that. I'm not going to bring it up.

Back in South Carolina, the afternoon has just begun, and there's a decent chance no one will be around (they might be at the neighborhood pool or at the mall or wherever teenagers go when they have freedom), but E answers the phone and peppers me with questions, most of which I can answer with a single word, which is a good thing. The second I hear her voice break through the hiss of international static, I lose the ability to construct complete sentences for a few seconds. *Are you guys having fun? Did you buy me some stuff? When are you coming back? Where's mom?* She has no idea what's barreling down on her. She's the oldest. She'll have to guide her sister through whatever emotional maze springs up when we get back to the States. I immediately wonder about her tiny size and if the future will be too big for her. The thoughts catch bone-like in my throat.

"Dad?" she says when the silence goes on too long, and I consider telling her everything, about how her mom is leaving us all and how the world will pitch and lean in a different direction very soon. Rationale is a just a cheap drug. It can convince you to do idiotic things at the worst possible moment. Like shatter a kid's world using an international phone card. Telling E that her mom is leaving is simply a way for me to avoid the face-to-face meeting, the eye-to-eye encounter that is inevitably coming, the moment when her mother sits her daughters down and explains that she needs space, that she needs time—the same kitchen speech I heard a few weeks ago.

"You still there?" she says and snaps me out of the trance.

"We fly back in two days," I say, gathering up some enthusiasm in the heat. "We're having a great time."

Maybe I sound like I mean it.

TRENTADUE.

Those two days drift by. We easily ignore each other at poolside. (There are no more invitations to prove my daily passion, either on the pool deck or in the bedroom in the villa. I've obviously flunked that exam.) Our friends depart for the airport at different times, and the villa turns intimidating in its new silence. We leave early one morning for Florence and the airport. The highway wavers in the heat, even though it isn't yet ten o'clock. Since the dinner in Serra, we haven't spoken more than a dozen words to each other, though we spend nights in the same bed. I've quit trying to create small talk. Silence has become the norm. If a conversation were to break out, neither of us would know how to react.

We shove dirty clothes into the crevices of our luggage, cramming souvenirs for the girls into any empty space we can find. She insists on wrapping the bottles of olive oil she's purchased with dirty clothes, then wedging them deep in her suitcase. Images of oily shirts and broken glass flicker across my imagination, and I start to protest, then stop. It's not my problem, not my business. Not anymore.

I stop to fill up with gas near the airport, before we return the rental car to the steamy parking lot outside of the customs entrance. She sits in the passenger seat, the air conditioning still blowing on her while I fill the tank. As I watch the numbers cascade over the top of one another on the pump, I attempt to calculate how much of this trip has gone to her side of the ledger and how much to mine. I'm already beginning to divvy up expenses, already starting to try and hoard what little I have of my own. I wonder if this is healthy? Or natural? Or clichéd? Maybe this is the beginning of scar tissue, the way to cope with the inevitable pain, this contemplation of the mundane things, like who will pay for liters of petrol.

I have some trouble getting the cover to latch over the tank. The cheap plastic clips don't seem to line up correctly. I think the rental car went on my credit card, too. In fact, I can't think of much that didn't go under my name. The goddamn flap won't close, no matter what I do. She knocks on the window and points to her watch, as if I have lost the ability to keep time. I can't figure out what's wrong with the flap. I mean, the gas tank is closed; I've screwed the cap back on. I'll bet I've paid for this whole fucking trip. I'll be stuck holding the tab for Italy. I'll be drowning in Euro bills, suffocating from the exchange rate. I don't know how all of this works. Who gets stuck with what? She sticks her head above the roof from her side and says that we need to get going, that we have a plane to catch. I tell her to shut up and it's the first harsh thing I've said to her since that evening in the kitchen when she said, "I have to leave, I have to get going, I have to get going."

Goddamn things that won't work, that won't fit, that don't seem to have a solution, no matter how carefully you try to fit them back together. I've become careless. I pull too hard and the cover breaks off in my hand and I'm standing there with a piece of the fender in my palm. I think about throwing it, about winging it as hard as I can toward the back of the gas station. She looks at me through the window and sees what I've done and she laughs. I can't hear her through the window, but I can tell she is laughing at me. When I climb back in, it's quiet again. She's had her laugh, I suppose. The only sound is the air conditioner hissing at us. I toss the flap into the back seat and downshift into traffic. I go faster than I probably should, but we don't want to miss the flight back home.

TRENTATRÉ.

Inside the Galileo Airport, the immigration officer gives our passports cursory glances. Nobody seems to care when we arrived. Nobody cares that we are leaving. The attendant at the gate doesn't even flip through the pages and search for our arrival stamp. Nobody cares about anything. The heat has sucked the desire out of everyone who works at the airport. We pay a penalty for her overweight bag—more Euros on my card, mostly for her bottles of expensive olive oil that lie buried deep among her shirts and dirty underwear.

Normally, I love the feeling that washes over you once bags are checked and tickets punched, the relief of having taken care of the details. All that is left is to sit and wait for the miles to begin whizzing by. This time, however, relief is the farthest thing from my mind. I watch the minutes until departure tick away and I feel like a prisoner, a dead man walking. Since no one knows about the looming thing, I have no hope for a reprieve. In fact, the only sensation that overtakes me is one of failure. The clock has, indeed, run down to triple zeroes. I couldn't save this, couldn't pull it out before the buzzer sounded. My game plan was faulty. Maybe I should have been angrier, broken more things with my hands. Maybe I should have pestered her with questions, kept her off-balance with a steady barrage of dialog. Goddammit, I was too quiet, too passive. Too *passionless*. And now it's too late. I sink into the seat at the gate, making myself smaller. When you fail, you want to shrink, you want to become quickly invisible.

She, on the other hand, is giddy. She flips through entire magazines in mere minutes, snatching the pages with a moist index finger and shucking them machine-like to the side. She buys more magazines. (At least that's something that I'm not paying for, I think.) Her feet bounce on the carpet. Her eyes dart toward every sound. I haven't seen her this anxious, this *aware* in weeks. She points out things in the magazines— pictures and paragraphs and numbers—and I want to tell her that I don't care what is happening in the world outside of my own. But that's the world she wants now, the one she can't wait to step into, the one outside of mine.

Trentaquattro.

I'm not sure what to tell you about the flight. We simply shift our seats from the gate to the narrow aisle on the plane. I keep trying to make myself smaller and smaller, working on my disappearing act. She continues to fidget, the energy pouring out of her. We don't talk unless it is necessary, and it is unnecessary most of the time. There is a movie, but I can't tell you the name of it. There is music in the headphones, and all of the songs seem to be directed at me. Love is being lost, heartbreak is drifting down in the headphones. I have to turn it off, finally.

I start to watch the monitor over the seats that displays the map of the Atlantic Ocean. A tiny cartoon plane makes its way in the direction of the east coast of the U.S. Numbers flash regularly, telling me how fast we are going, what the temperature is outside of the airplane and how long it is until we reach Atlanta. The little cartoon plane is inexorable. It crawls non-stop along its thin line toward home.

Once, I wish for the plane (the real one, not the drawing) to drop out of the sky. It's only for a split second that I want this, and the thought of coming to an end in the Atlantic scares me. Ending that way, right here and now, would certainly make things easier for me. And it would ruin her plan, whatever that is. But the thought of never seeing my girls again makes me nauseous. The two of us being apart will hurt them, sure. But the two of us being gone forever might kill them. Then, of course, I concoct a scenario in which only I survive. I see the rescue and the reunion. And I never tell them that their poor, drowned mother was about to leave them to find her *space*.

IV.
PRINCE ALBERT AND
THE DIVORCE SANDALS

35.

In Atlanta, the U.S. Customs Agent finds it hard to believe that no one stamped our passports when we first arrived in Italy. I try explaining how lax everyone tends to get over there, especially when it's hot. I even ask him if he's been to Italy.

"This shouldn't happen. 9/11 changed things, you know," he says.

He contemplates calling over a supervisor, but decides to let us back into our own country.

"Wouldn't that be crazy," I say to her, "if they didn't let you back in? What would you do then?"

I'm not sure she even hears me. She is busy digging her cell phone from the depths of her large purse and checking to see if any battery power remains. Her eyes light up.

"I'll call the girls and let them know we're back," she says, angling toward a bathroom.

"In the bathroom?" I say. She just waves off my question as if it were stupid and ducks into the women's room. I pace outside the entrance for minutes and minutes, waiting for her to return. I wonder how much she is telling the girls. I don't want her stealing the good stories from the trip, the few that I have, then I chide myself for wanting to divide up our stories like they were common property. We'll do enough of that later.

She returns smiling. "They said welcome back and they love you," she tells me.

"Long conversation," I say back, more edge in my voice than I intended.

"What is it with you?"

This time I don't answer her. I let her words hang in the air, not because I'm dramatic, but because I don't have a short answer. I'm questioning everything because I under-stand nothing. I have thousands of questions for her. Yet I have none. I want to know everything she is thinking and feeling, but I don't. I'm scared. I feel like tomorrow is the first day of first grade and I'm in a new school and I don't know a soul. I'm alone. Or about to be.

The horn sounds for the arrival of the bags and the crowd does its little surge forward. A man brushes into me slightly—no big deal—but he apologizes profusely. He wears a gaudy Hawaiian shirt, but instead of palm trees and pineapples, his is decorated with stars and stripes. I glance around and see American flags in every direction, t-shirts with Uncle Sam spread across the front, even a Statue of Liberty hat on a teenager. I've been gone too many days, with my head buried in the sand of her leaving. I didn't realize.

"It's the Fourth of July," I say. She nods.

We've come back from Italy, so she is leaving me. We've touched down on Independence Day. I'll bet she knows exactly what day it is.

36.

In mid-July, she sets her time-table. She will leave mid-August. She makes plans she doesn't share, writes more lists I'm not allowed to see. I do know about the Lyle Lovett concert. She wants to see him play again, in a week or so, and she wants me to take her.

The pressure I felt on my shoulders in Italy increases, presses down harder when she buys the tickets to the concert. The ache in my knees increases from the new weight. Lyle Lovett. The two of us grew up together on Lyle Lovett. In my first year of teaching (and the first year of our marriage), one of my more musically progressive students— named Ross, I believe—brought me a cassette one morning: *Pontiac* by Lyle Lovett.

"See what you think about this. It's wild," Ross said, tapping the plastic on the cassette cover. I didn't know if *this* meant the music inside or the dramatic yet somehow manly beehive hairdo on the photo he tapped. "It's not what you expect." And since I wasn't expecting anything, it was indeed a surprise. His music was like his hair, all over the place, corkscrewing into areas that weren't country, weren't pop, weren't Texas Swing. And yet, the music was all of these things at once.

She and I listened to *Pontiac* together and loved it. We made our own copy of *Pontiac* and wore out the tape. We followed Lovett's progress and his tours and bought whatever he released through the years. We saw him live again and again, in Atlanta and Charlotte and Asheville and Greenville. We made our children listen to him in the car.

We cooked dinners with Lyle in the background. We rolled our eyes when he married Julia Roberts.

Now, as she's making her exit, she wants to see Lyle Lovett one more time, in a town thirty miles down the interstate. "I'll buy the tickets," she says, suggesting she has already begun dividing things into the two new categories: hers and mine.

I have no desire to see Lyle Lovett a few days before my wife leaves me. I mean, I feel as though I've become the subject of a country song, one of his songs. I don't want to go anywhere with her, but she insists. "It will be a good thing for us to do together," she says.

She has a therapist now, and I sense her therapist there, the hand up my wife's back, moving her mouth like a ventriloquist's dummy. My wife would never think going to see Lyle is a good idea right now, but somebody making $100 an hour to concoct painful tasks might.

But Italy broke any resistance I possessed. I keep my mouth shut. "If you're not interested, I can get a friend to go with me." I can't let a *friend* sit beside her at a Lyle Lovett show. That would put a wobble into the earth's orbit. I agree to go and hate myself for that, but self-hate is becoming as familiar as a first cousin.

We drive the thirty miles mostly in silence on the evening of the concert. Though it's after seven o'clock, the parking lot bakes in July heat, car engines pinging as they cool down. The show is sold out and the lobby of the auditorium crawls with people buying one last beer before the lights flash a warning. Despite the crowd, she immediately spots two of her friends—tan, fit runners who comprise part of her regular Girls Night Out Group, eight or ten women who get together every couple of weeks.

My wife is all smiles, greeting them with hugs and squeals like sorority girls after summer vacation. Her friends, Ellen and Sharon, are already in mid-concert form. They laugh about drinking in the parking lot and not noticing the cop peering in their car window. I've known Ellen for years. Our children grew up together. Sharon is a stranger. I've heard of her, but never met her. She erupts with a constant enthusiasm, flitting into our conversation hummingbird-like, then darting away for a few minutes. She hovers between excitement and boredom.

I can't pretend to be happy. This concert, like the next month, the next year, is simply another event, another chunk of time I want to get through as quickly as possible. With a beer, I down a small handful of Ibuprofen I brought in my jeans pocket, hoping to lighten the load on my knee. Ellen looks at me, probably wondering about my self-medication, as Sharon bursts back into our little circle.

We file into the auditorium to our seats. Lyle is accompanied by his Large Band—I can tell from the collection of music stands and chairs onstage. Ellen and Sharon sit elsewhere in the auditorium. I look around for them, try to catch a glimpse of Sharon's energy one more time before the lights go completely dark. I tell myself: If I ever get through this, that's the kind of energy I need to be around. That feels healthy.

Lyle's hair is smaller than his *Pontiac* days, some seventeen years ago. *Seventeen years. I've been married seventeen years.* An odd thought there in the dark.

When the music begins, I'm immediately angry. She is trying to ruin this for me, trying to put a black asterisk in my memory, beside Lyle Lovett's name. She is taking everything she can gather up before she leaves, and the anger is somewhat of a relief, like a pinprick in an air mattress, letting off tiny jets of pressure that no one really notices.

Lyle sends his Large Band offstage for a break, and he is left under a narrow sliver of spotlight, accompanied only by his cello player. He dips into *Pontiac* and moves to more recent albums, songs I know by heart. And I feel it happening, coming too quick for me to stop, feel it rising from my chest, a sad, sour nausea settling in my throat. I begin to cry in the dark. *Seventeen years.* We rocked babies listening to Lyle Lovett. *Seventeen years.* We unpacked boxes in new houses listening to him. Breathing becomes difficult. I want to ask her why she brought me to this, why she put me through this, but I can't find a voice. She leans over. "What is wrong with you?" she says. "You're embarrassing yourself." I hear a quick snort in my ear.

Seventeen years. I don't remember the rest of the show.

37.

I reach the point of begging. I'm not sure why I haven't tried sooner, but there I am one night—in the kitchen again— saying whatever I can think of to keep her in the house.

"Stop it," she says. "You know what would happen if I stayed?" Then, she pauses. It isn't rhetorical, but I don't have an answer. When I visualize her staying, I see more grinding and muddling, more looking for answers. I see work, but at least I see her here, under this roof. I know enough not to tell her that, so I remain quiet. She answers for me.

"Nothing," she says. "That's what would happen. Absolutely nothing. Because you never listen. You never do what I ask. It's just like those goddamn sandals."

I know exactly what she is talking about. The Bata sandals from Italy lie in my closet. I haven't worn them much since we'd returned on Independence Day.

I've dubbed them the Divorce Sandals. The day I bought them, a group of us from the villa caught the mid-morning train to Florence to spend the day exploring, roaming shops and museums and the outdoor market. But an hour into our daytrip, she wanted to split us up. She had an errand for me. "We need cash," she said. "Can you go to an American Express office and get some money? I think there's one only a few blocks that way." She waved in the general direction of the Duomo. I knew I could find the location of the American Express in a guidebook so I didn't care which way she pointed. My friend Steven offered to go with me. His wife would stay with mine, shopping and wandering, making plans for the money I was withdrawing. We would reconnect in an hour.

Steven and I headed in the direction of the American Express office, but after a few blocks, a shoe store caught my eye. I can't recall why this particular store turned my head, probably because the shoes were expensive. Maybe it was the tall Italian woman rearranging the display in the front window. Perhaps it was the cold blast of air that spilled onto the sidewalk each time someone left or entered. Whatever the reason, Steven and I walked out of the heat and into the rows of Italian shoes.

The saleswoman looked like a runway model, like Monica Bellucci. She didn't smile or greet us. She simply walked toward us, sneering a bit, daring us to ask her to do something. "Damn," Steven said. She was dark haired, dark eyed. Her shoulders, bare in the dress she wore, were broad and tanned. She didn't give a shit what we were thinking. She didn't care about anything but selling us shoes. And we let her.

There was no conversation. I'd simply point at a shoe. She would eye my foot, then disappear into the bank of cold air and return with a pair that more or less fit. She never asked me for a size. Never wanted to know how something felt. Steven sat to the side. (With a wave of his hand and a shake of his head, he'd let her know he wasn't buying today, and she turned all her attention to me.) He was happy watching her. I was happy trying on expensive shoes and letting her touch the heel of my foot.

Finally, she began to smile and talk. I didn't understand a word, and I told her I didn't, but she continued. From the inflection in her voice, I could tell they were questions. (Oh, and the voice. A purr crossed with Lauren Bacall. I didn't care what she asked me, as long as the questions kept coming.) I realized how long it had been since a woman had smiled at me when she asked me a question. Of course, I knew she was trying to get me to reach for my wallet. But it didn't matter. It was nice to have a conversation about something other than leaving and daily passion and the end of things, nice to have a conversation even if I couldn't understand a word.

I turned my attention to a display of sandals, probably because I could afford them. I pointed at a pair in the window and her eyes lifted a bit. She returned with the pair of Bata sandals. I slipped my bare foot into one of them. The sandal wrapped around my foot like I'd been wearing it for a year. "*Va bene*," she said, and I understood. She knew these were the shoes I should buy. I gave her my credit card at the counter and told her I would wear the new sandals. I started to put the old ones in the box, but she interrupted. She did it for me, tucking soft paper around my old running shoes. She handed me the receipt and smiled and I smiled back, both of us happy with the way the transaction went down.

Steven and I walked into the heat and almost bumped into our wives. The good feeling from the shoe lady had spilled onto the sidewalk with me along with the cool air. I smiled. "Look," I said, pointing at my feet. "I got some sandals."

She waited a second before answering. "So you've been to the American Express office?" she asked, already knowing the answer.

"We're on the way now," I said. I wanted to walk in my new sandals.

I watched her boil behind her eyes. I saw her contemplating how angry she would get in front of our friends. She decided she didn't care who heard her when she began to yell.

"That's what I mean! That's exactly what I mean! I ask you to do one thing, just one thing, and you don't listen. You don't care about what I want. I asked you to get us some money and you buy shoes. Does that make sense to you? This is what I'm talking about. You don't listen. You just do what you want to do."

The Italians on the sidewalk didn't pay attention to her. They were used to loud conversations. But the tourists looked at her, and looked at me. Especially the Americans. They knew something bad was happening. Steven and his wife didn't know how to act, so they turned their eyes away, trying to figure out which direction to walk. Or escape.

When she stopped, I said I would go get the money now. "It's no big deal," I said.

"It's too late," she said. "Forget about it. You had your chance." She wasn't talking about money or sandals.

38.

Kitchen conversations now, if they occur at all, begin to take on an air of either desperation or insanity. For instance, while I'm standing at the sink rinsing dishes, she tells me her therapist feels as though I should create a plan for her exit. "She says you should come up with something you are comfortable with," my wife says. The idea that I should create the logistical bullet points for my wife's exit strikes me as lunacy.

"Why the fuck," I ask her, "would I plan something I don't want to happen?" This seems like common sense to me, to avoid pain, to pull your hand *away* from the stove when you feel the heat of the red eye.

"She thinks you should do it," she answers without flinching.

I dry my hands. "You're going to do this, right? You're going to leave." She nods. I'm not surprised. I know the answers already. I'm just setting up. "Then you figure it out. You're a smart woman. And tell your therapist I said to bounce up my ass."

Though I don't believe in therapy, I have already offered it up as a possible solution, a last gasp. I suggested the two of us go see someone. "Right," she said when I mentioned it. "I'd spend all of the time working on you. It would do me no good." For her, there is only one solution and that is to run away. That's been settled.

She just doesn't know how to do it. She doesn't want to be the bad guy. She doesn't want to appear to anyone—her children, her friends, her therapist—like the woman who pulled up the marital stakes, folded the tent and fled into the night. She wants a list that takes her through the process of imploding her family, and when she checks off the last task, she wants to feel pure and clean and guilt-free.

Which is why she insists I be the one to tell our children. (She gives credit for this idea to her therapist as well. I'm beginning to wonder if this therapist even exists. If she is real, I can't believe my wife is paying for this type of advice.)

She tries crazy angles of rationale. "Do it for me," she says, like I owe her debts I can repay by blindsiding my children. (They *still* have no idea this is coming. They think life is moving at normal speed toward a normal destination.) This, I know, is not something I should do. I'm not good at these kinds of conversations. If I could write it out beforehand and create everyone's dialogue, I'd be fine. But having to work by the seat of my pants, not knowing what the reaction will be, not knowing who will say what—this mystery leaves me cold and afraid.

I realize I'm not going to fix this, so maybe she is correct, maybe I should participate. I see what she's doing. She doesn't want her children to remember The Day Mom Told Us She Was Leaving. She wants the opposite. Let dad do it. Perhaps our kids will think since I'm telling them, I'm okay with it. Who knows what she's thinking? I'm no therapist. Thank god.

39.

I magine the worst day of your life.

It will never be as bad as the day I gather our daughters and herd them into the sunroom. (I cannot do this in the kitchen. That room has been damaged enough in the past few months.) She follows us in, a little paler than normal, but very much in control of herself.

E and M sit on the couch, like prisoners about to be interrogated. I see them trying to figure out what's going on. They glance at each other as if to say, *What did we do wrong?* But they have no idea what is about to happen. They think they are about to be scolded for leaving the back gate open again and letting the dog escape to the neighbor's pool. E thinks her driving privileges are about to be revoked. M, always the one to assume guilt even if she did nothing to earn it, imagines she's about to be accused of armed robbery or shooting an animal.

I feel my eyes filling, and my children notice. This scares them immediately. They've seen me cry before, in movies or at a funeral, but never in the sunroom, never on an evening when nothing bad has really happened. My wife sits away from me, in a chair on the far side of the couch. Her jaw is set. She's had time to practice her stoicism. I haven't rehearsed a thing. I spent my energy hoping this moment wouldn't come, trying to change the outcome before the clock ran down, hoping that by some miraculous twist of fate she would change her mind. (I know. My own brand of desperate insanity.) I look at her now, her eyes dry and darting to avoid making contact for too long with anyone in the room, and I realize there is one thing I cannot do: I cannot tell my children the truth, cannot tell them that one evening their mother stopped me in the kitchen and said she is leaving. I cannot tell them about Italy and the eggshells and the clock running down. I cannot tell them about Lyle Lovett. I cannot point a finger at her. I've thought about it, considered how I might emerge from this conversation blame-free, more heroic than simply sad. But I glance at her and I think, *Seventeen years.*

I look at the children we made and I know I have to say the right thing, which is, "This is not a good conversation. I have to tell you something." And I do. I tell them what is happening, what will happen, and I fill the air with clichés and they float like heavy balloons around the room. I say things like *grown apart* and *need space* and *still love each other, still love you* and *not your fault.* I talk until I can't talk anymore, until the words catch like something sharp and low in my throat and tears come instead of sounds.

They cry with me. I'm not sure they've understood anything I've said, which is okay. It makes no sense anyway. I gather them up in my arms. They are not too old to hug, but they have grown so big, it's hard to hold onto them at the same time. E whispers, "I'm sorry," into my shoulder and my heart heaves into pieces. I wait to feel my wife join this hug, to feel her add her arms to this painting, but she never does. I turn my head slightly toward her and she still sits in her chair, her legs crossed, eyes dry. She hasn't shed any tears for this.

I sense her therapist in the room somewhere, like an expensive ghost, and I want to choke the both of them.

40.

August in South Carolina is a month when little moves, when it's too hot for people or animals to do much more than breathe and drink and eat. The thick humidity is a constant, milky haze in the sky, as if a huge fire burns nearby, and all we get is the blanket of smoke. The air smells musty, like it's been shut up in an attic for years. This is when she chooses to leave, a scorching Sunday afternoon in August.

Since I refused to come up with a custom-made plan, she handles the logistics herself. She has lists in her hand, things she must remember. "I'm not taking much," she says. "The new apartment is so tiny." She sounds excited, shaking her lists, putting things in Seagrams and Jack Daniels boxes I hadn't noticed. She must have gone to a liquor store when I wasn't looking.

The children have driven to a friend's house because they are hiding. They know today is the day Mom moves out. They haven't asked questions. They haven't talked about it much at all, other than to shrug and say most of their friends have divorced parents, like they've suddenly contracted a common disease they'd miraculously avoided for years. *Seventeen years.*

I've made plans as well. I'm going to be gone when she packs up. I have no desire to see the process of furniture leaving my house. I don't want to watch her decide which pictures to take off the wall. Her brother-in-law is driving up to help her move. He is a very quiet man who smiles most of the time. And he's very religious. He will see the hand of God in this somewhere. I may end up in a bar, although the options on a Sunday in South Carolina are very slim if you're looking for a stool and a bartender/therapist. I might drive into the mountains and find a place to park, somewhere near water, where it will be cooler.

She gets calls on her cell and ducks into another part of the house to talk. When she returns, she begins packing again. Once, I hear her humming. I'm searching for my keys when another call comes in. It's her brother-in-law. "He's broken down on the interstate," she says with the phone to her ear, her eyes widening. When she hangs up, she rattles off a story, something about a snapped axle on his trailer and bearings that have burned out. I'm not really listening. I'm watching her. She's suddenly manic, pacing the borders of the narrow kitchen, talking to no one in particular, especially not to me. The talking turns to a level just shy of screaming. "This cannot happen! I have to do this today. I have to leave today."

If I were trying to make her stay, if I thought there was any time left on the clock, I would smile at her and say, "See? This is an omen. You're supposed to be here." I would make a charming joke out of it. But I've given up as much as she has. I want her gone, too. I just don't want to watch it happen.

I'm pissed at her brother-in-law. He's making things harder on me. She's crying now, distraught that she can't begin finding herself and enjoying some new space on a Sunday afternoon like she'd planned. Her lists are no good now. I don't know whether to stay and enjoy her frustration or leave for my ride in the mountains.

She looks at me, wide-eyed and crying, crumpling the lists in her hands. She says again and again that today has to be the day. I can tell she wants this night to be the first one away from me. She needs my help, and the thought of it makes me laugh, which confuses her because she has yet to think of me as a solution for her Sunday Dilemma. I am literally seconds from leaving, keys in my hand. Without saying a word, I take the phonebook from the cabinet under the kitchen counter and look up the number for the U-Haul dealership just down the road which is, like I suspected, open until six on Sundays.

She doesn't understand. "I can't drive a truck," she says. "I've never done this." Everything she says is fat with subtext. I walk to my car, and she finally understands. "I'll pay for this, of course," she calls after me, and I think, We're all paying one way or the other.

I'm not angry until I hit the bends in the road on the way back to my house. The panel truck steers like an aircraft carrier and the engine, when it tries to accelerate, shakes the cab until my teeth rattle. It was the last truck in the lot.

"You're lucky," the girl in the U-Haul uniform told me when I signed the rental agreement.

41.

You can never prepare for the feeling you have when you carry your own furniture out of your house, furniture she takes as she leaves you.

42.

The two of us sweat, working together to slide bed frames through a tight doorway or bend a loveseat around a corner. The heat makes everything—the physical effort, the anxiety, the anger—worse. The cement driveway is a stovetop, and the dark insides of the truck are broiling. Each time we carry a piece of furniture up the metal ramp, I sense the wall of heat before I step into to the black space that we slowly fill. We soak through our t-shirts, working together like this. Other than "right" or "left," I haven't said a word to her. I don't want her to recall anything but silence and heat when she remembers this day.

She takes very little. Just a couple of things off the walls. She wants to come back later and decide how to divvy up the artwork. (We don't own expensive art. It's mainly stuff we bought for each other on Christmases or birthdays. It means something, though.) The U-Haul is barely half full, the pieces of furniture secured to each other with some ropes I have in the garage. I don't know where her new place is. I follow her through the neighborhood and we cut across to a busier street. A couple of our neighbors stand in their yards, hosing down their shrubs, and they wave when we drive by, not realizing they are telling half of us goodbye.

Her new apartment is a duplex just over a mile away, a small two-story place on a quiet street, on a steep hill. The apartment is laid out oddly, tiny rooms broken up by strangely located doorways and false walls. The building is owned by one of her friends, so I assume she gets a good deal. And it strikes me that someone else in the world knows about this. I haven't said a word to any of my friends yet. I haven't figured out how to do it. (Do I make phone calls? Or just let it come up in conversation? Email?)

We struggle with the furniture in the narrow spaces. Symbolically perhaps, the pieces that fit so well in our house have no room here. I rake the skin from my knuckles trying to guide the bed up the thin staircase. The chairs make the small den seem Lilliputian. It bothers her, I can tell, but she makes the best of the situation by talking, which angers me. I am happier with silence.

"I think this will work," she says. "I can put the round table here in the kitchen and the coffee table will just barely fit here, but that's okay, I don't really use it that much anyway..." And she continues a monologue about absolutely nothing until the doorway fills with another person, a stranger, a woman.

"Oh," my wife says, "hello neighbor!" She is too cheery. I know how false it sounds, but no one else would pick up on the hollow tone. They've obviously met before. Another thing I didn't know about, another confidante. I put down the box I'm carrying. I don't feel like being nice to anyone, don't feel like giving anyone any measure of respect. I'm not required to do that today, the day I move my wife into her escape. I drip sweat, waiting.

"This is my husband," she says, motioning to me.

Her neighbor sticks out her hand and I dumbly take it. *Her husband.* She could have just said my name. But she gave me a title, the one I've held for seventeen years. *Seventeen years.* If she had just said my name, I could have been anonymous. I could have been just a friend helping out. I could have been a brother-in-law who didn't break an axle. But I am the husband. For a split second, I'm buoyed by the way she introduces me. She hasn't taken that away from me yet.

But I look at her and there is a smirk on her face. I understand: She has put me in my place, in a new place. Yes, I am the husband, the one she is leaving, the one who is sweating his balls off to move her out. *Hey neighbor,* she is saying, *can you believe it? I'm leaving and this pitiful bastard is doing all the work. For free.* I feel like a chain gang convict, standing there, dripping sweat on her floor. I want to run, but there isn't room.

We empty the truck and I can't recall if I told her goodbye. I drive the truck as fast as I dare on the road back to the U-Haul dealership. In a couple of places, I feel it tipping slightly on the curves. Wrecking would be okay, but I don't want to die. That's something, at least.

I pull up to the U-Haul dealership just as the girl is locking the door. It's six o'clock, straight up. She smiles at me. "Just made it," she says. "You're living right today."

43

She wants everyone to be happy. She wants us to smile and hug and not point fingers at her. She wants to live without guilt, and I don't blame her. I'd probably want the same things. That's why she takes the girls to Target to buy them stuff for their new room. (Not *rooms*. Her new apartment has only two bedrooms, so she must bribe a pair of teenagers with new sheets and wall hangings and drapes.)

The girls aren't pleased with their new accommodations. They want what is familiar and gives them plenty of space to lose themselves. But they love their mother and they realize (or at least they've been told) that this is only temporary. She is planning to buy a new house with plenty of bedrooms as soon as she is able. The girls tell me how, in the mornings, they fight over space in the single bathroom. E tells me sometimes there isn't room to park her beat-up Volvo in the back. They tell me about watching the lesbians in the house next door, drinking wine on their back deck. They seem to think it is relatively cool and urbane to live in such close proximity to lesbians.

A couple of weeks after I help her move in, she calls and invites me over to the new place. Not a social invitation. "I want you to see the apartment now that we've settled in. I want you to see where our daughters are living half the time." Her use of *we* turns me nauseous instantly because it's a group I'm not a part of. And there are other reasons she wants me to see her apartment. She thinks I should know how well she is doing without me, without us. She wants me to bear witness to her quest to find new *space*. Or maybe she just needs me to know that she is okay. I can't decide. These days, motivation is a fuzzy subject. Confusion has been keeping me up at night. On the periphery of her voice, I detect a hint of pleading, so I tell her I will be there that evening, but that doesn't work for her; she has plans. I'll need to come tomorrow.

I smell fresh paint when I walk through the door, and things are in place, in order, not like the only other time I was there, sweating and stacking furniture and boxes against walls and in corners. Seeing her apartment is like spotting a stranger on the street wearing clothes that belong to you. It's foreign but vaguely familiar, a brand of violation, not a violent one, but a violation nonetheless. She's stuck lists to her refrigerator with magnets that she brought from the old house. I know those magnets. Late summer tomatoes sit in the kitchen window sill. Drifting under the paint smell is something she cooked last night, a sauce with lots of spices. The children weren't at her house the previous night. They were with me, and it quickly twinges my heart that she is cooking for herself and eating alone at the small, round glass table in her kitchen.

"This won't take long," she says, laughing. "Not a lot to see." She herds me from the kitchen into the tiny den where she's set up a television in front of the couch that used to sit in our spare room. The last time I saw the couch it was shoved against the far wall. Now, the couch eats up the space, leaving barely enough room to maneuver to the staircase. We head up the stairs and the paint smell fades enough to let me take in her scents on the landing: perfume and soap, hair and skin.

"It looks nice," I say flatly, not unlike a prospective buyer, wandering through a house for sale, not wanting to let the broker know how much I love or hate the place.

The girls' room is just as tiny, with two single beds bordering the outside walls. A single dresser is littered with earrings and bracelets and nail polish bottles and CD cases. I have to smile at the fact that my girls have left their fingerprints on a new space in a matter of days.

"That's it," she says, and I follow down the stairs. From

above her, I see that she's had her hair done recently. There are new streaks of blonde among the darker blonde, and any sign of gray is gone. She bounces down the stairs like she knows them. Back in the little den, she asks me if I want to sit down. "I've got beer," she says. "At least, I think I do."

I can't stay. I'm not that civilized. I can't perch in her new life for too long. I don't want to be exposed to its atmosphere. I make one last glance around the room, taking things in, so later I can imagine where she is, where she's standing, where the girls might be walking. I notice on the little side table a blue-and-white VHS case from Blockbuster. She doesn't see me reach down to turn the spine. *The Good, the Bad and the Ugly*. Eastwood. A classic. A Western.

I hold up the case like I've discovered a relic in an archeological dig. She finally sees what I have in my hand, and there's a rush of something, perhaps panic, behind her eyes. The paint smell grows stronger, instantly.

"You hate Westerns," I say, more confused than anything else. I recall an evening years earlier when I came home from Blockbuster with *Pale Rider* and she refused to watch it. Back then, she said, "I don't like Clint Eastwood. Plus, you know how these stories end a quarter of the way through."

I start to remind her about *Pale Rider* and her dislike of Clint when she interrupts me. "No big deal," she says too quickly, "I'm trying new things. Not so unusual."

That night (another night when my mind races, trying to catch the blades on the ceiling fan whirring above my head) I am amazed at how big of an idiot I am.

Now I know there is someone else. Someone who appreciates Clint Eastwood. Maybe he likes the way she did her hair. Maybe he enjoys her cooking.

Then I tell myself, *No, she wouldn't do that*. It's about needing space and time. Not about dinner and Westerns.

44.

My house expands with her gone. When the girls aren't around, which is every other week, the walls move back and leave me with too much space to occupy. I mean, the house has always been big—a long, one-story brick ranch built back in the '60s. Five good-sized bedrooms and three full baths. We used to joke that the house is so long, it has two zip codes, but it isn't ostentatious big. Rather, the house at 47 Stono Drive is a lumbering relic from a time when people valued things like walk-in closets and rooms large enough to roller skate in.

We bought the house to make things easier for E. After each of her limb-lengthening surgeries, she spent a lot of time in a wheelchair and on crutches, so a one-level house seemed a logical move to make, especially since our previous house was built into a steep hill, and E was getting too big for me to ferry up and down stairs. But now, everyone walks just fine. There is no carrying to be done. Every other week, I find myself sitting alone in big rooms, listening to music. Music is the sound I want filling up the house. I load five CDs onto the tray in the stereo, open a beer and find a place to sit. I change rooms every evening. And I stay inside. I haven't been able to go to the pergola yet. I don't even know if the birds are still there.

This is my way of sorting things out. I have to decide what is really worth worrying about. I need order. I even consider making a list, but that feels too much like her. I have lawyer worries and money worries. I have email duels with her about visitation and child support. I worry about the anger and the spite.

Shadowing it all, at least for me, is somebody I've never seen, the man who likes Westerns.

45.

She actually makes an appointment with me, to decide which pieces of art she wants to cart to her new apartment. I don't recall an overabundance of wall space at her new address, but she insists we divvy it up. This is the unofficial division of property, she says. Her lawyer is taking care of the rest.

We don't have what you'd call an art collection. We've never had that kind of money. But we're friends with a lot of local artists and we worked deals with them, trade-outs, gifts-in-kind, etc. There are some nice pieces, but the value of the things hanging on the wall is mostly sentimental.

She wants to stop by in the late afternoon, which is prime worrying time for me. I can't call it happy hour, but between five and seven, I load up the CDs and sit in half-empty rooms. I decide not to alter my pathetic routine, so when the doorbell rings (which seems immediately odd, her ringing her own doorbell), I'm halfway into a six-pack and a tray of music.

She is shopping, I think. She wants to wander through the house and pick out what strikes her eye. She smiles and wants to chit-chat like regular people, like pals. I can't. I won't even try. Having her inside the house shrinks the rooms the moment she walks into them. I don't even detect the echo when she talks, the empty reverberation I've heard for weeks now. I follow her through the ranch-style maze of our house, watching her study the walls. Finally in the living room, she stops.

"Oh, I'd like that," she says, pointing at a painting, a

portrait of a woman wearing a red scarf around her hair. The woman in the painting is dressed very conservatively, a blouse buttoned to her throat and a dark sweater or coat wrapped around her. It's difficult to detect the details of the woman; the brush strokes are loose and the indistinct colors mottled. My wife bought the painting for me as a birthday present years earlier. The fact that she wants it back raises bile in my throat.

I croak a bit when I remind her. "You gave me that," I say.

"Yes?" It's a question. She stands between me and the painting, and she looks fit, like she's been running, her dancer calves tighter than usual. I'm betting she hasn't been spending *her* fall evenings sitting and drinking and winding her way through trays of CDs. She's waiting for an answer, but I have begun to cry. I can tell she thinks the tears are a strategy, that I had this little art collection breakdown planned. I didn't. In fact, I want to tell her how unexpected my reaction is. All of the worrying and the beer and the evenings in the expanding house have banded together and come at me, full force. She sneers.

"Well, I can't do this if you are going to cry," she says, turning quickly down the hall toward our old bedroom. She calls over her shoulder. "I'll come back when you're more stable." She continues to talk in my direction, telling me she'll take one thing now, a charcoal sketch of a woman sitting on a bed, gazing out a window at a horse. The only reason we bought it is because the woman in the sketch looks exactly like her. It seemed cute and funny at the time, so we hung it on the wall.

She passes me, hugging the piece awkwardly against her. "Can you please get the door for me?" She winds through the garage and tosses the frame on her back seat a little more roughly than I would have liked. But I won't miss that piece. The last thing she says to me is, "What the hell are you listening to?"

Later that evening, when I'm far deeper into both the CDs and the beer, I push the button and the tray slides out. The CDs stare up at me. Damian Rice's first album. Two different Elliot Smith selections. This thing by Mark Kozelek—slow,

brooding versions of old Bon Scott-AC/DC songs. The fifth
slot is blank. I couldn't have possibly picked bleaker music.
This has become my soundtrack.

That night, I turn off the stereo. I sit in the large silence
of the house, which probably isn't any healthier, but at least
no one is singing at me, telling me how bad off to feel. I can
do that all by myself.

46

One Saturday afternoon after I watch a mountain stage in the Tour de France—the tiny climbers burying themselves in pain on the switchbacks—I decide to buy a bike. Then, I do something that borders on psychotic behavior. I call out to my empty house: "You mind if I go out and spend a shitload of money on a bike today? That okay with you?" I put a hand to my ear to catch the response. "No?" I holler out. "Well good, then. I'll take that as a yes."

I watch the Tour every July. I love the expensive bikes, the insanity that hovers over the crowds in the mountains, the pain on the faces of the cyclists. When I watch the races, I remember being twelve. I lived in a town with very few hills, only a few minor bluffs that fed into the Black River. My Uncle David bequeathed me an old commuter bike of his, a Schwinn with tall, thin tires and a handful of gears. I had my father trick out the bike with a banana seat and high-rise handlebars, creating an odd hybrid, a cycle only Frankenstein could love.

My friends and I—a little pack of twelve year-olds—would head out on summer evenings after supper, around six-thirty or so, and wouldn't turn for home until the light had faded, close to nine o'clock. We'd ride to the river and take a hard-packed dirt road into the tobacco fields on the flood plain. We'd circle by the Moose Lodge and turn back for town, short-cutting by an old tobacco barn where the high school kids parked and made out and drank beer. We knew where the dogs would charge out from the Ligustrum hedges that bordered blind driveways. We knew how to avoid the teeth-rattling train crossings. I would pull into home sweaty, my legs turned to unfamiliar jelly, and sleep like a dead man, sometimes in my clothes, on top of the bed spread.

In my thirties and forties, every time I watched the Tour, I remembered those nights, and every summer I vowed to try and get them back. And why not? Why wouldn't I want to get that sort of freedom again, the freedom that comes from keeping my legs pumping, the wheels turning?

For a number of years, in July, I would tell her I was going to buy a road bike, and each time I asked, she had a reason to make me hesitate. These involved either what she viewed as the inevitable idiocy of riding a bike in traffic (I couldn't blame her. She worked in a traumatic brain injury unit and saw the foggy survivors of bike accidents on a weekly basis) or a shaky financial investment. "I don't think we should spend money on that right now," she said more than once. "Maybe you could look for a used bike or something?" I stopped pleading my case after a few years. She would not understand my attempt to recapture the sweaty, exhausted feeling from my days on the Frankenstein bike. She was too practical for that sort of nostalgia.

Now, the first July after she leaves, almost a year since I loaded her in the U-Haul and moved her into that new space she so desperately wanted, I sit in the living room and watch men with oversized thighs and overdeveloped lungs chew up pavement in France. The events of the past year have left me addled to the point I have forgotten what I enjoy doing. The Tour has reminded me.

The closest bike shop is less than a mile away, housed in a half-domed Quonset hut, probably left over from the '50s. I walk in Sunshine Cycle and straight to a guy behind the counter, a tiny little man with close-cropped Brillo hair. He reeks of superiority and boredom, but I don't care. I'd heard cyclists can be that way. If you aren't in the club, if you don't know the secret handshake, you can't get in the door.

He says, "Yes?" without looking.

"How do you get paid?" I say.

He glances up. I've got twenty years and thirty pounds on

him. And today, I have a look in my eye that I haven't had in months, at least not since she left. I am flashing the do-not-fuck-with-me look.

"What do you mean?" he asks back.

"I mean, do you work on commission? Because if you do, this is easy money. I'm not walking out of here without a bike and helmet and shorts and shoes and you're going to take care of everything for me, right?" I say, and as a nice punctuation mark, I slap a credit card on the counter. He immediately becomes my best friend for the afternoon.

The next morning, I leave my house early before the people and their cars are up. It's Sunday, so I point toward the country, away from the traffic that will scatter toward churches in a couple of hours. I begin to learn the gears and try to remember what the guy at the shop told me about shifting. I'm like a prisoner in shackles with my feet clipped onto the pedals; it feels too intimate to be that attached to a piece of machinery. The helmet is a bit bowl-like on my head and already the saddle bisects my ass, and there is, after forty-five minutes or so, the unnerving feeling that my penis is falling asleep. But I haven't been this happy in a year.

On the slight downhills, the bike leaps out like it is trying to become airborne, and the speed makes my toes curl inside the new shoes. I learn how to stand out of the seat on the grades and rock the bike up the hills. I haven't felt like this since I was twelve and sweating and cranking through tobacco fields on the edge of my hometown.

I see her one afternoon when she comes to pick up our daughters. "Did you ever find a therapist?" she says, as if therapy is an unavoidable side effect of divorce.

"I did," I say. She wants to know who I'm seeing. "He's very specialized," I tell her. Specialized is the brand name of my bike, and it has, indeed, become my therapy. Every hour I spend on the bike, tapping out a rhythm up a hill or slinging around a corner, I count as an hour I don't have to pay some guy to tell me that my feelings are natural and my anger will fade. I don't really want my anger to fade. It makes me pedal faster. When I leave my house and take off for a climb up the backside of Paris Mountain, I know I will

Scott Gould

feel better that night. I'll pull into my driveway, sweaty and smiling and I will sleep like a dead man again, like when I was a kid. And whatever chemical I am producing that burns my legs and fills my brain with a warm fog will wash through me and carry away a little bit more of her while I sleep.

47

So she left on a hot August afternoon. I stayed. In a big house with a pergola out back and a new bicycle leaning against the wall in the spare room, leaning there daring me to ride it. And the days flowed by until they became quickly months, then years, then time didn't seem to make that much difference, no matter how long or short it took to pass. The girls grew up. They stayed with me every other week, and in the week I didn't see them, they changed. Just about the time I caught up with the changes and committed them to memory, E and M disappeared for another week and I lost track. It was strange and awful, parenting in intervals.

Because my advertising job was eating me alive from the inside out, I went back to teaching at a local arts high school and writing my own stories. I told myself the new job would give me more time to write. But my free evenings—when I should have been putting words on paper—found me under that pergola, fishing beers from the cooler between my feet, listening to the wrens I'd disturbed in the Crossvine. I ate out a lot, mostly at Tito's, a local pizza and pasta place where the owner and his brother spoke Italian. I'm not sure if I went there for the food or to hear the language that I couldn't understand.

I began to lose my hearing, too. The doctor diagnosed it as garden variety tinnitus. A constant test pattern hissed between my ears. I remember the moment it happened. One morning, a couple of days before she moved out, I woke up and my ears filled with the sound of haze, and the sound didn't go away. I kept making appointments with the ear, nose and throat doctor, and he kept telling me, "Well, you're not deaf yet," and I thanked Dr. Obvious and paid him and wondered why? Why, at a time when I needed to be listening harder than ever, at a time when I needed to hear everything around me clearer than ever, did my ears begin to ring?

48.

A nd then:
One morning, a woman called me at work. This was when I was still slogging through the advertising business. She told me her name and asked me if I knew who she was. I didn't recognize anything coming through the phone. And I never enjoyed these sorts of mystery calls. I said I hating guessing at things. She told me she was married to the man that my wife had been seeing. "The man she left you for," she added. That's when I went quiet.

My stomach lurched in my throat while I walked to a room where I could listen without anyone watching me. In those few steps, I remembered what my lawyer said one afternoon: that when a woman leaves you to get some *space* and *find herself*, ninety-nine percent of the time, there's a man already there on the outside, waiting on her. I was convinced he was wrong.

The woman's voice tumbled through the line, non-stop, as if she'd rehearsed all she was saying and was afraid she might not be able to spill it before I hung up on her. She said she'd known about the two of them for a long time. When she finally had proof, she'd moved out of her house, taken her kids with her. She talked about timing. She said it was funny that my ex-wife moved out not long after she did. The woman on the phone said she wanted to talk in person.

"I travel for my job. I'm going to be in Spartanburg this week. Can you meet for dinner? I have some questions to ask you." I immediately thought this was a bad idea. But I also knew I couldn't pass up the chance to hear this story.

We set up a time and place, and before she hung up, she said she would fax me some phone records.

"I work for a cell company. The idiot didn't think I could get to his records? Anyway, you'll see what I mean," and she said goodbye.

I waited by the fax machine for five minutes, pretending to be on the phone, wasting time, so no one would wonder why I lingered near a quiet machine. Finally, it chirped and pages of phone records curled out, calls from his number to my wife's, hers to his. There was a call from her on July 4th, about the time we landed in Atlanta. And short calls on Sunday mornings, probably as she left the house, just to let him know she was on the way to see him. Never on the way to Mass.

But it really is a test.

49

I wasn't sure what to expect. I had no preconception about her looks or her hair or the way she walked, yet when she came through the front door of the restaurant, I was, for some reason, taken by surprise. Probably because she looked nothing like my ex-wife. She wasn't blonde or long-waisted. She didn't have a Roman nose. Her face was open and attractive, but not striking, and she wasn't smiling uncomfortably like I was. I wanted friendly. She wanted all-business.

The awkwardness was thick and unavoidable, and once we'd been seated and given drinks and left alone, I gave up on attempting small talk. "You told me you had some questions," I said. I noticed she was a blusher. A wave of red began to creep from her shirt collar up her neck.

She said she had two. The first one: Was my ex-wife bisexual? To keep from appearing too stunned, I made a joke, said something like, "Only in my wildest dreams." The second question was equally surreal: Did we swing?

By now, the red wave had worked its way to her ears, and I was afraid she might faint. But the fact that I answered *no* to both of her questions seemed to bring on a sense of relief. She took a sip from her wine which gave me a chance to catch my breath as well. I knew it took a lot of effort and moxie to ask a perfect stranger those questions. She actually smiled. She'd crossed a hurdle.

"You see, if you'd said yes, then I'd know why things went wrong for us," she began. "He wanted me to do things. And I wouldn't and he turned into somebody different. I thought maybe he'd found somebody who would, you know."

Then she launched into a story that seemed to have

multiple beginnings. She was heading somewhere with all the little tangents: about him asking her to bring home lovers so he could spy on them from the closet. About him emptying the garbage cans into the trunk of her car because she supposedly threw away his can of smokeless tobacco. (While she was confessing her secrets, the only thing I could think was: my ex-wife left me for a man who dips?)

I didn't know where the stories were leading until she finally said, "And then one afternoon, he comes home with...a Prince Albert."

The look on my face told her that I had no idea what a Prince Albert was. She smiled again, when she realized that she still possessed information that I didn't. Then she told me about a Prince Albert. About how it's the slang name for a penis piercing. She tried to explain how the piercing worked. She pantomimed with her hands where the u-shaped stud was inserted and how the ball ends kept it from slipping out. She talked about how proud he was of it, how he put up with the infection and the blood and how hard it was to pee. She was making fun of him and didn't even realize it.

She drank more of her wine and began to enjoy herself. "I had to leave. I couldn't let my daughters be around that," she laughed. She had a pair of daughters, just like me. She ordered dessert when she finished her story.

My ex-wife. She left me for a man with fishing tackle on the end of his prick. I didn't know whether to feel better or worse.

50.

On the drive home, I wanted to call someone and tell them—
holler into the phone—that my wife had run away with a
man who could set off a metal detector with his crotch. I had
never laid eyes on this man, The Other Man, the guy who
liked Westerns and watching his own ex-wife wrestle with
strangers, the man who liked to slide a pinch between his
cheek and gum. I knew something about him that he didn't
know I knew. I felt like I suddenly had an advantage. He
may have her. But I know a secret.

Since the initial phone call from the woman, her
ex-husband had always been, in my imagination, six-four
and chiseled like a Greek god. His shoulders to his thirty-
inch waist formed a perfect vee. He could put women into a
coma with his skill in bed. He *had* to possess these charac-
teristics for me to be able to sleep at night.

But now, this was different. Jewelry dangled from his
penis and he reeked of Skoal. He cruised websites at night,
searching for neighborhood sexual swap meets. He was no
longer the Greek god. He was a crazy little dude with a u-bolt
in his pecker. I didn't feel bad for my ex-wife. I would never
be able to squeeze out that sort of empathy again. I thought,
no matter how bad it gets, no matter how many lonely CDs
I listen to and how many miles I pedal, I will never poke an
extra hole in my dick.

I didn't call anyone. I just drove through the night, singing
the songs that came on the radio, already writing the scenes
in my head, the one where I happen to run into The Other
Guy in a bathroom somewhere and over the urinal, I ask
him, "Hey, you still sporting Prince Albert there, buddy?"

51.

I found Antonluigi's envelope under a stack of shoeboxes high in the bedroom closet. *5 Ottobre 1943*. It had taken years, but now I had the time (and I suppose, the desire) to read about Guilfoil. His story was in the envelope. Once I opened up the papers and started to read, I couldn't put the story down. The sheets of paper were nothing more than Air Force reports, slivers of cold and detached data about the flight that day the plane went down. As I read, I began to insert details without really thinking about it, began the process of giving the story texture. These papers were the skeleton, and I started putting meat on the bones.

In early October of 1943 a B-17 nicknamed the Rhomar II, full of men and bombs, left Tunisia, North Africa in a formation of flying fortresses on a bombing run across the Tyrrhenian Sea to Bologna. It was a long flight, hours there and back. According to the flight plans for the mission, the weather that day was clear, a crisp autumn day in Italy. One of the men in the belly of the B-17 was young William Guilfoil, a nineteen year-old from Chicago, a wiry wisp of a guy who, in photos, always has a cigarette hanging from his lips at a rakish angle, as if he's trying too hard to look older and cooler than he really is. Guilfoil was the tail gunner, a dangerous position at best, dangling there on the farthest extreme of the plane, watching the air he'd just left behind, seeing what might be gaining on him.

The only attack the crew of the Rhomar II faced on the way to destroy the Bologna rail yards came from boredom. Sleeping was next to impossible, even if you didn't have a job flying the plane. Conversation was limited because of the incessant drone of the engines.

The return flight was a different story. After dropping their payload of bombs, the Rhomar II turned back for the coast and flew into a patchwork of German anti-aircraft shells that exploded around them like fireworks, puffs of smoke and metal. Guilfoil had nothing to shoot at. Before the pilot could take the Rhomar above or below the corridor of flack, the plane was struck several times. Shards of metal sprayed inside the plane, and several of them struck Guilfoil in the face and head. Suddenly, he was the blind tail gunner. Despite feathering the remaining engines, the pilot couldn't keep the Rhomar aloft; the damage was too severe. The plane dropped below the cloud cover, abandoning the formation, and made several wounded circles around the tops of the rolling green mountains northeast of Lucca, hovering closer and closer to the chestnut trees that blanketed the countryside.

The crew, already strapped in their parachutes, bailed. All except Guilfoil. He was too bad off to save. He couldn't see the faces of his friends when they made the quick decision to let him go down with the Rhomar. It was the right decision. A chunk of Guilfoil's skull was missing. He couldn't see to crawl from his gunner position to the belly of the plane. He was beginning to black out for a few seconds at a time. I imagine him babbling things only he knew, places in Chicago where he used to eat dinner. The names of Cubs infielders.

Nine chutes opened over the valley, some of them attracting German fighter planes that zipped in for a fly-by mop-up. The German pilots could have sprayed the men dangling there with machine gun fire, but most of them didn't. A couple fired some shots just to show off. They knew the floating Americans would eventually come to solid ground and be gathered up alive—a more valuable commodity than dead.

The Rhomar crashed south of Serra Pistoiese, into a thick forest just off a two-rut cart path that led to a spring the villagers used for their drinking water. Guilfoil rode the Rhomar into the chestnut trees, shearing off their tops, and coming to rest, amazingly, belly down and mostly in one piece. No explosion, no ball of fire.

The people in Serra watched Guilfoil crash to earth. They saw the smoking plane circle their village. They prayed out loud for the plane to find some place to collide, other than their tiny village. They saw the parachutes balloon into life and watched the men twisting below them. They heard the plane slam into the forest. They ran down the cart path, toward the spring. For the people of Serra, curiosity was one of the few things they still possessed that the war had not dulled. Everything else—hope, love, ambition, happiness—had turned gray and become more of a memory than a real thing.

The villagers beat the local *Fascisti* to the crash site. The plane had survived remarkably well. The wings were still attached and the crash had somehow extinguished whatever small fires had been burning onboard. Other than a few places where the trees ripped small holes in the fuselage, the bomber was intact. The metal hissed and crackled as it cooled, and the Rhomar lay there like some gigantic, prehistoric forest creature that had settled down to die.

The adult men stepped closest to the plane, the young boys hiding behind them, peering around their fathers and uncles at the B-17. Finally, one of the men looked inside the fuselage and saw Guilfoil, dead and slumping against the side of his tiny turret, still trying to look older and cooler in his blind, blank death-stare. His uniform was smoking a little, and the smell of hot flesh filtered up toward the branches of the chestnuts that had withstood the crash.

Several men pulled Guilfoil from the plane and laid him softly on the forest floor. Most of the people had seen a dead body before. Death was no mystery to them. They stared as the *Fascisti* arrived, some on horseback, all of them carrying guns—shotguns mostly—that had been drafted into the war from their places above the mantel.

There was an argument. The Fascists wanted the plane to remain untouched until the Nazis showed up. And they wanted to carry Guilfoil into the forest and dump his body. "Let the wild boars, the *cinghiale*, have at him," they said.

The villages were tired of being told what to do, especially by men who were brave only because they had a shotgun under their arms. They stood their ground. They surrounded Guilfoil like a pack of angry animals. They told the *Fascisti* that Guilfoil would be buried in the village cemetery. He would be given respect, the respect the dead deserved, no matter where they were born, no matter what uniform they wore.

The Fascists shook their shotguns in the air. They made noise. The villagers didn't move. Guilfoil's body cooled. The villagers won. And the Fascists rode away, still shaking their guns at the sky, making the empty rattling sounds they'd perfected since the war'd begun.

52.

I wanted to simplify my world. I took a job that didn't give me nausea every Sunday evening, anticipating Monday morning. I stopped taking tiring vacations. I bought a beat-up used Nissan Pathfinder that was cheap and reliable. I started drinking Pabst Blue Ribbon beer. These things, I thought, were the makings of a simpler life. But I was still living in a huge, echoey house. I couldn't rid myself of that because I was too lazy to get it ready to sell. Every time I mentioned moving, my daughters begged me to keep the place they'd grown up in—though they only slept there every other week. The house was the looming thing now, the weight that pressed down on me.

When I found out about Pierced Penis Man, I stalked through all of the rooms and removed any sign of her. I flipped through every photo album and threw away pictures of her. Sifted through the junk drawers and got rid of her hair ties and bottles of nail polish. When mail came addressed to her, I didn't even check the return address before I tossed the envelopes in the garbage. I told myself, *Leave if you want to, but don't expect me to sort your mail.*

Yet the house stood as a constant monument to my failure, and the fact that I had to pay monthly for its existence infuriated me daily. It struck me one evening, after a long, sweaty bike ride, while I cooled off under the pergola: Now I wanted revenge. After all of these months, I didn't want her back. I just wanted to get back at her.

Maybe it was because I was still a competitor. My failure during the trip to Italy had not dulled the edge of that particular character flaw. Maybe it was sudden appearance of Pierced Penis Guy. Whatever the reason, I still wanted to win in the worst way. It had been awhile since I'd won anything. A couple of days after I had my post-ride epiphany, I received a brochure from the Surdna Foundation. Even though I don't believe in omens and portents, when I read the brochure, I shivered like an animal had run across my grave, like something strange and magical had occurred.

53.

They passed out brochures from Surdna to the entire faculty
at my school. When I read the words, here's what I heard
them saying to me:

Hey Scott!

*Here at the extremely prestigious Surdna Foundation, we
have caught wind that you're looking for a way to get
back at your ex-wife, to stick it to her, to make her feel
something other than the apparent complete and utter
happiness in her new life with the guy who possesses a
pierced penis. And while this revenge motive seems a
lame-ass goal to have in life, we are here to help you.
We give fellowships to teachers at public arts schools
around the country. Nice, big, juicy fellowships. All you
need is a legitimate project that will further your devel-
opment as an artist. We'll give you five grand to finance
that project. "Getting Revenge on the Ex-Wife" is not an
apropos project, however relevant it might feel. On the
other hand, going back to the little village in Italy and
researching that tail gunner—what was his name? Guilfoil?—certainly smacks of legitimacy. You see, Mr. Gould,
you could travel to Italy on our proverbial dime, do a
little snooping around in Serra about Guilfoil, then write
a short essay about your adventures. Easy peezy. A few
hundred words of jingoistic fluff. Meanwhile, you could
spend the bulk of your valuable time trying to sully your
wife's reputation among her extended family. After you*

get through with her character, she will no longer be the blond American quasi-celebrity with the Tuscan nose and the pidgin Italian. Nossir! She will be the One Who Fled. The One Who Left The Pergola. Her branch on the Italian family tree will begin to wilt and lose its leaves. You will have a final, hearty laugh, Mr. Gould, and we will pay for it. All you have to do is write up that whole legitimate part, you know, cross all your t's and dot all your i's. Make it sound better than it really is. (You were in advertising. You can do that in your sleep. Wink wink.) Convince us that you're going to accomplish something worthy. Once you arrive in Serra, how you conduct yourself is completely up to you. We will not be there, peering over your shoulder. You'll be on your own, sir.

Good luck and godspeed.

54.

Of course, I was hearing things. Surdna's brochure was pretty straight forward. They did, indeed, give fellowships to arts teachers at public arts high schools. You could fit the number of public arts high schools on a relatively short piece of paper. In other words, the odds of getting a few thousand dollars from the good folks at Surdna were relatively high if you taught at a public arts high school. If you possessed half a brain and knew how to pitch an idea, the odds were even better. If you had a good idea for a project, knew how to pitch it *and* happened to be an arts teacher at a public arts high school, you were close to a sure thing.

My idea had a lot going for it: the Great War and accompanying war heroes, stereotypical Nazis, overzealous Fascists, the Italian countryside, humble villagers. I didn't think there was any way they could ignore me. What I didn't tell Surdna wouldn't hurt them. They'd get an essay about Guilfoil and the brave villagers and the story that Serra couldn't let go of.

I'd get an all-expenses paid trip back to her roots, and I'd be stoked on revenge. Win win.

55

As I filled out the Surdna application, I thought about lies. Antonluigi, the rich man with the poor dentures, could have been telling me a fair number of untruths, decorating Guilfoil's story like a birthday cake, adding flourishes of icing each time he thought he saw me stifle a yawn. (Did the Fascists *really* carry guns? Was Guilfoil's body *really* smoking when they pulled him from the plane? Was Antonluigi's memory *really* that sharp?)

I have always feasted on stories that were probably lies. I remember my grandfather lifting us grandchildren onto his cracked recliner and telling us about the semi-pro baseball league in Alabama, where one afternoon he actually pitched to Ty Cobb. He recalled specifically the time he covered first base on a ground ball to the right side of the infield, and Cobb spiked my granddaddy's Achilles "for no good damn reason at all. Cobb was out by three steps. Bastard didn't need to hurry." I got older and checked to see if Cobb played in Alabama or if my granddaddy pitched in the league. The dates didn't match up. All lies.

When I was a little kid, at suppertime the standard dinner question from my father was, "What happened today?" My answer usually involved a Western scene, horses and outlaws. I recall telling my parents stories about riding into town and helping the sheriff clamp down on a gang of outlaws who'd wandered in earlier that afternoon. I remember that I was constantly a fast gun. And my parents *believed* the details I made up. Or rather, I believed *they* believed the lies. The bigger the lie, the better. I was praised for making shit up.

Scott Gould

So maybe Antonluigi added something here and there. What was the harm? Maybe when I applied to the Surdna people, I added a little bit more. Who's going to get hurt by that? Guilfoil's mythology was growing, at least in my mind, and he'd been dead for more than six decades. Now, I could talk to people and find out the truth. Their version of the truth, that is. What they think they saw. Or something they'd heard so much about so often, they actually believed they'd been there. The fictive nonfiction. The nonfiction lie. Just more outlaws and bandanas, only this time in Italy.

And I'd be exporting stories to Italy. The ex-wife stories. I couldn't predict how many I'd want to tell when I arrived in Serra. I could mention to Paolo how, just weeks before our last visit, she'd said she was leaving me when we got back from Italy. I could tell him how she turned into a blue-movie star in the Tuscan hills, somebody giving me orders from the bedroom, ones I couldn't decipher. I could tell him how I'd discovered, quite by accident, that she'd been having a *relazione amorosa* with a guy who sported a pierced penis. (The penis I'd never seen. I only heard a story about it. Or a lie about it.) Those were all good stories.

I imagine some of them might have been true.

56.

From: " ████████████████ " < ████████ @surdna.org>
To: <sgould@ ████████ >
Subject: Surdna Arts Teachers Fellowship

Dear Scott Gould,

Congratulations! I wanted to notify you as soon as possible that your fellowship application has been accepted and you have been selected to receive a Surdna Arts Teachers Fellowship.

The award of this fellowship is pending formal approval by the Board of Trustees of the Surdna Foundation in early May. The Foundation requests that you not contact any press or media until you receive official notification of your fellowship. You may certainly tell your school and colleagues. Immediately following the board meeting you will receive a formal notice and a contract for your award, as well as materials to assist you in making a public announcement.

As outlined in the application, to process your Fellowship contract requires that you submit:

- documentation of acceptance or confirmed plans for the fellowship venue you have selected or applied to;
- written confirmation from your mentor (if part of your project) outlining the specific terms of your mentorship (dates, times, etc);
- a schedule of your travel/study plans if completing an independent study project;

- confirmation of your teaching appointment for the next school year.

If you have yet to supply this documentation, please do so as soon as possible. If you have already provided this material, there is no need to resubmit. All materials must be received no later than June 30. Fellowship funds will be distributed by the end of June, but not until all required materials have been received.

Once again, please accept my congratulations. Feel free to contact me via this email, or, at 212-███-████, ext. ███

57

The knee was still a problem. I had begun walking like an old, old man, struggling and shuffling each morning to get from the parking lot of my school to my classroom. I couldn't imagine handling the inclines and cobblestones and switchbacks in Serra on a knee that grinded away with every step and ached around the clock.

I tried everything, anything. I had a minor surgery before the trip to clean out some of the gunk in the joint. That worked for about a week, then the creaking and grinding returned, just as bad as before the surgery. A doctor with a bow tie gave me a series of shots that was supposed to lubricate my joint. The main ingredient in the miracle lube was rooster comb. I asked him how somebody discovered rooster comb was good for lubricating knee joints. He laughed at me. "Smart farmers, I guess," he said, pleased at his improvisation skills.

The shots didn't work. Not a bit. It was just additional pain, with a needle that felt the size of a number two pencil. I told the doctor I just wanted to be able to walk around Italy, and he laughed and spit out some poorly accented Italian greeting, then proceeded to tell me about the trip he and his wife made to Italy the previous summer. "Rome," he said, gazing dramatically at the ceiling and holding the fresh needle like a conductor's baton, "Rome is very historical, you know?" I told him I wasn't aware of Rome's history and thanked him for clueing me in to such an under-the-radar concept, all the while keeping my eye on the needle that danced between us.

Each time I went for a shot—I had four sessions of them—he told me something new and exciting about Italy. Like how there were no streets in Venice. *No streets at all!* And that the shoes in Milan were very expensive but worth every penny. (This was when he pulled off one of his soft, brown loafers and tossed it in his hand like a baseball. "This shoe won't appear stateside for another year, I'll bet!" he said.)

Neither his shots nor his cultural history of Italy made me any more prepared or excited about leaving on my trip. The final solution, at least the only one possible in the amount of time I had left, was pharmaceutical. The doctor with the expensive shoes offered me a brown paper bag full of high-powered Ibuprofen and a prescription for a bottle of Lortab. "Don't drink any *birra* or *vino* with these, ha ha!" he said, tugging on his bow tie and ripping the prescription off his pad.

I looked at the prescription and did some quick math. He'd written it for thirty pills. At what I guessed would be a reasonable rate, that would translate to around one and a half a day. This seemed to suggest hours of unmedicated pain. "What if I run out while I'm there?" I asked.

"How long did you say you'd be gone?" he answered.

Again, quick math. "Three months," I said. This was I lie I deemed necessary and completely justified. I was only going to be in Serra for about three weeks. I wanted, I said to myself, to be completely free of pain and able to concentrate on the task at hand in Italy. I wanted to be able to interview those people and walk the hills without limping. Hence, the lie.

"Oh, my," he said. He stared at me a bit too long, calculating the odds that I might actually be a pill-head with a bad wheel.

"I just want to enjoy the history of Rome without worrying about my knee," I said, casting my gaze longingly toward his loafers, looking as pitiful as possible.

"Certainly," he said, tearing up the prescription and writing another for close to triple the amount. I left the doctor's office feeling somewhat like a Lortab addict, even though I'd never tried the stuff. "*Buongiorno!*" the doctor said, smiling above his bow tie.

58

The people at my school were pleased I received a Surdna Fellowship. I filled them in about Guilfoil and the story of the plane going down, but I didn't mention my ex-wife's Italian family and the paper bag of Lortab stashed in my bathroom cabinet. I told my daughters, almost in passing, that I was returning to Italy, to Serra. They complained (once again) about not being included in the plans, but their hearts weren't in the protests. They were too busy with their own worlds at this point. Truthfully, the reason I told them about the trip is so they would spill the news to their mother.

I sent emails to Serra, to Silvia the daughter, who possessed an actual email address. They were short messages, in simple Italian, explaining when I would be coming and why. I didn't mention a divorce. I guessed they knew nothing about it. I *hoped* they knew nothing about it. I received one answer from Silvia, one word. "Yes!" she wrote. That was enough to convince me that they were fine with the plans I'd laid out.

The night before I left, I sat in a chair under the pergola and listened to the wrens rustling in the vines. Only June, but the nights were already hot and humid, hints of dog days ahead. I waved at mosquitoes and tilted a beer bottle toward my face. I had taken a Lortab a half hour earlier, the first from my stash. It seemed smart to self-medicate ahead of time, before I had to fold myself into an airplane seat for six or seven hours. The pill began to take effect. The pain in my knee turned suddenly less dull, now more of an annoyance, like the mosquitoes buzzing my ears. The world lost its sharp edges for the moment. There was really nothing to worry about. The Guilfoil story would unfold. I would have wonderful dinners with Paolo and his family, where I would talk in fluent Italian. (Lortab, I decided, would magically grant me the ability to speak a foreign language.) I would tell my ex-wife's distant family dark, revealing stories about her behavior and they would ban her from Serra in perpetuity. *This is going to be fun*, I told myself.

I wondered if she knew I was leaving the next morning, wondered if she cocked her head at some point and asked herself: *Why the hell is he going back there?*

I hoped she was thinking about me and it was keeping her awake.

V.
Ghosts and Angels in Serra

CINQUANTANOVE.

GHOSTS AND ANGELS IN SERRA

My flight landed in Florence during the blazing part of a summer afternoon. I limped across the familiar sticky parking lot to the rental car trailers, found my diesel Volkswagon in the heat and pointed it west. I staked out a spot in the slow lane on the Autostrada, giving myself some time to re-acclimate to the speed of Italian driving. Before I hit the exit to Lucca, I turned more north toward the mountains and spent a half hour meandering through Montecatini Terme, searching for the road into the hills. The first stage of what would become a pattern emerged that Sunday afternoon: On this trip, I would often find myself lost, take a couple of wild guesses, and magically discover the correct direction. I don't recall looking at a map during the entire trip. It happened first in Montecatini. The heat and the fact it was a Sunday had kept the streets empty. That was lucky. I could drive slowly and search for landmarks, for anything that pointed me toward Serra.

I wasn't panicked. I knew the general direction. I mean, I could *see* the mountains to the northwest. I drove in low gear through the tight, maze-like neighborhoods and into blind alleys. I couldn't find reverse in the gearbox once and ground the transmission like a blender. Couples flocked around an open gelato store, nuzzling each other. I only saw one bar open, on a corner where a couple of bright-colored Vespas leaned against a stone bench and old men in straw hats drank something clear out of stubby café glasses. They waved when I crawled by. They thought I was hopelessly lost, and they grinned at my predicament. But they were wrong. I was moving, I was making my way to the mountains. I was something resembling happy.

The sun settled low and brilliant on the side streets, blinding me through the windshield and my sunglasses. Okay, I was lost but it felt good. Oddly safe somehow. I saw a soccer stadium I recognized from years ago, and I skirted its edge, veering toward the hills. The sign for the Parco di Pinocchio appeared suddenly on the shoulder of the road, and I knew, *I remembered*, that I should turn left before I came to the giant carving of Pinocchio and begin winding my way toward Serra. The sides of the road started to look familiar. I magically knew which turn to take at crossroads.

I wondered how much I would remember about Italy, about the previous trip with her. Or, rather, I wondered how much I'd forgotten. I supposed that was the same thing, this remembering and forgetting, or remembering *to* forget. There was no way to prepare myself for the recollections that would surely rise to the surface. No map for that either.

SESSANTA.

The ride up the mountain spread into something familiar. I recognized the layout of the hairier switchbacks. The road to Serra climbs almost twenty-five hundred feet out of Montecatini Terme. The narrow, shoulderless two lanes bend and eat their own tail again and again, playing tricks with gravity. In the past, this road served as a stage for the famous Giro d'Italia bike race, and I imagined thin, feather-light cyclists bonking when they hit a switchback, struggling to keep their bicycles upright. The rental VW possessed a decent lower gear, and I roared around the switchbacks faster than I should have.

At a certain point, signs—real signs, not omens—began to point to Serra, though I didn't need them. I knew the way, felt it somewhere in my head or in my hands. Steering became easy. I stayed in that one gear, riding the clutch a little. I was the happiest I'd been in months, humming along, staring out over the hills when I wasn't watching the road.

Late Sunday afternoon in Serra, an hour before complete darkness. Men and women gathered in the square-that's-not-really-a-square outside of Paolo's ex-hotel. Most of the men wore felt hats, even in the dwindling heat. A half dozen people played a card game at the wicker table near the open door of the only café in town. Some smoked and blew clouds over each other's shoulders. Two boys in sandals kicked a soccer ball against a wall of the apartment building that had been a convent decades ago, and a tiny girl, a sister maybe, spectated from the top step, clapping when something good happened.

I spotted a parking space in front of the café, ten yards from where Paolo sat on a bench. I recognized the shock of salt-and-pepper hair and the achingly familiar nose. And he wore those odd glasses, the kind with lenses that darkened and lightened automatically. The sun had almost dipped behind the buildings, draping the square with the dull tones of a sepia photograph. The people stopped what they were doing and watched me like I was a fugitive they *almost* recognized. The sound of the kicking ceased. No one dealt the cards. Strangers in the village were big news.

Paolo stood as I opened the door of the Volkswagan, backlit by the remnants of the afternoon sun. He stared for a few seconds, one hand rising to his mouth. He had his Mayor-of-Serra look on his face, the Protector, the One Who Will Question the Stranger who just pulled into town. Finally, a hint of recognition flickered in his eyes.

"Scott?" he asked. "Ciao, Scott?" He didn't trust himself to recognize me.

"Si, ciao Paolo," I said and saw realization wash over him. He remembered I was coming. He just hadn't known when. There had been a miscommunication, an error in the oddly worded emails. But I'd made it. And here I was, just before dinner, not as lost as I'd seemed.

SESSANTUNO.

Paolo didn't ask me to eat with the family that first night. I imagined Renza staring and glaring him out of an invitation, so after we greeted and made plans to meet later, I coasted back down the mountain a few kilometers to a pizza place I'd spotted on the way up. The jet lag began to seep into my bones and my brain, and I limped more than usual. I blamed that on the long, cramped flight and the fact I hadn't popped a Lortab in six or seven hours. In fact, I couldn't remember where the bottle was. My little bottle of miracles.

After dinner, I found my way back up the mountain to Serra and parked the VW at the edge of the dark and empty square. I didn't spot Paolo in the shadows until he called to me from his bench. He waved me toward his house, and I picked my way carefully across the uneven stones of the street, followed him into the light and sat at his kitchen table.

The whole family gathered there, waiting. I remembered the layout from my last visit three years earlier: a front room that blended into a small, yellow dining room. Just off the dining room, a claustrophobic kitchen stacked with ancient looking appliances—like the charred and chipped gas stove that probably saw its best days just after World War II. A few steps from the kitchen, a narrow, granite stairway led to the upper stories, toward the halls of ex-hotel rooms. The frozen expressions of deer and wild boar still stared down from their taxidermied perches on the walls in the front room. Those walls were the most interesting, with the mounted animals and family photos and lithographs and posters of

Serra and of the mountains and of vacation spots. (I didn't know if they were posters of places the family *wanted* to go or places they'd already been.)

Among all of this sat Paolo's family: Renza the wife, Renza's mother Vivetta, Paolo and Renza's daughter, Silvia, plus a man I didn't know who was enjoying a cigarette far too much. He rolled the filter on his lips before every drag and when he blew clouds of smoke, he studied them like a fortune teller.

Renza smiled and waved me into a chair and poured me a small shot of limoncello without asking if I cared for any. Her hair was a lighter shade of red than the last time I saw her. Her eyes, calm and relaxed, studied me. Silvia gave me a hug and asked, in English, how I was doing. She spoke English as well as I spoke Italian, which was to say, we got by with moderate embarrassment. Vivetta, the tiny, silvery woman bent by age, was excited to see me because, I imagined, she recalled how much I talked to her three years earlier. I've always been more interested in people with the lines on their faces. Experience makes for better conversation. The family was a little surprised Vivetta had joined us. She'd been sick lately, bedridden for the past few days in her upstairs room.

Paolo introduced me to The Smoker. His name was Stefano, Silvia's fiancé. The wedding, they said, was in a month. In a machine gun rush of English and Italian, Silvia explained that the renovations of the ex-hotel were a result of the impending wedding.

Renovations, I thought? Then I recalled what I'd seen that afternoon through a fog of jet lag, seen but not really understood—scaffolding and plastic covering Paolo's house, a network of shrink-wrapped braces and plank platforms surrounding the exterior like a metallic spider's web. The scaffolding appeared delicate and lacy from a distance. But there were signs of heavier construction as well. Rusting electric mixers stained with cement and stucco, heavy rotary sanders discarded on the patio bricks, half-filled buckets of what I guessed was stucco, but looked more like tapioca pudding, drying and hardening in the afternoon.

She and Stefano were planning to live there, in a newly renovated room on the third floor. They told me Stefano was a lumberjack when he worked. (Lumberjack was my guess. The translation grew a little murky when Silvia described his job. I knew it had something to do with trees.) He looked too small to wrestle a chain saw and chestnut logs. Maybe he was management. His eyes were tiny, set way behind his glasses. When he offered his hand, I spotted the nicotine stains on his nails, and I never saw him without a cigarette the entire time I stayed in Serra. Even when he ate, one glowed in the ashtray near his plate.

Silvia wasn't faking her happiness. Her smile was genuine, quicker than I remember, usually followed by a giggle, her hair still a bright, unearthly shade of red. She'd lost some weight, no doubt for the wedding or the wedding dress or because of the stress. She was like her father. She liked to sit and talk. She didn't flutter and hover like her mother.

Paolo seemed to be waiting for something. I threw back another limoncello and felt it burn down and land somewhere among the three Peronis I drank at dinner. Somewhere in that soup, the Lortab I found in my backpack had already broken apart, making its way north to my head. The coffee sat on the table, waiting for someone to drink it, but coffee was no match for Paolo's homemade limoncello. He waited a fraction more, until Silvia poured another cold, syrupy limoncello into the small glass, then he cleared his throat and said, "*Che cosa è accaduto?*"

Silvia followed closely with a translation, but I didn't need it. He wanted to know what had happened.

SESSANTADUE.

Paolo wasn't angry. It was simple curiosity. He wanted to know why my wife, his fourth or fifth or sixth cousin—I couldn't remember which—was an ex-wife now. So, they had heard. They just hadn't been given details.

"Well," I said, "I'll try to explain." I nodded to Silvia so she could translate. I remembered how, years before, Paolo had used this same table to explain boar hunting to me. I could do the same thing, I thought. I stared at the salt. *I could be the salt*, but it felt too Biblical. Turned to salt. And pepper wouldn't work for me. I fingered the homemade hot sauce, the slim, unlabeled jar filled with olive oil and a mass of red peppers. Hot sauce was too—I don't know—too happy for some reason. Renza slid two cafés in front of us, along with a tin creamer and a tiny sugar bowl. *I could be the creamer*. That made sense in a weird way, the idea of being sort of plain and white. *Too easy*, I decided. I wanted to tell the story, but I didn't want to make myself the hero of my own tale. That is the worst thing a storyteller can do. But the creamer sort of made sense. Or perhaps it didn't. I couldn't tell any more.

I decided I would be the limoncello glass. That was my representative condiment puppet for the night. The ex-wife could be the hot sauce. Nothing symbolic in that choice, only that the bottle's shape reminded me of her thin, long-waisted frame. The Other Guy could be the pepper. I placed the limoncello glass and the hot sauce side by side. I pointed to the limoncello and said, "Scott...*capisca?*" Then I pointed to the hot sauce bottle and said, "*Spousa.*" I paused for a second to make sure they understood. I was the limoncello. She was the hot sauce.

Then, in cave-man Italian, I said (at least I thought I said, I hoped I said) that the hot sauce wanted a new life, a *nuova vita*. It was time to bring another character into the mix. I walked the pepper over and knocked the limoncello glass out of the way with the pepper shaker. The sound was too loud, I thought. I checked quickly to see if I chipped anything. "*Nuovo uomo, nuovo vita. Ciao, Scott.*" New man, new life. Goodbye, Scott.

Vivetta clucked her tongue, and Paolo nodded, then rifled off some Italian. Silvia said, "My father, he want to know when it happens."

"When what happens?" I asked. I was confused by the verb tense.

Paolo grabbed the pepper and lifted it in front of my eyes. "When *he* happens," he asked in crystal clear English.

SESSANTATRÉ.

P aolo wanted a time frame. He wanted dates. Actually, I wasn't completely sure. This was the current great mystery. *When?* My ex-wife had denied the early appearance of The Other Guy. But I possessed rumor and stories and tidbits of information. I had back-timed the appearance of the Other Guy to a certain month in a certain year, but who knew how long and how much? I gave Paolo the date I was positive about (I figured that was fair) and he began to do some math on his fingers. He raised an eyebrow and said something quickly to Silvia. Paolo was that rare Italian, quiet, with a voice that rarely rose. His hands lay on the table like small loaves of bread.

"What?" I asked Silvia. "What did he say?" She hesitated. Paolo nodded at her.

"My father, he says that he—" she pointed at the pepper— "that pepper man, was there when you visit us last time. You here with her. But he was there, also too? In her heart? I am making sense, si?"

"Yep," I said. The Lortab-Limoncello cocktail was in full effect. I couldn't feel my cheeks. The grind of bone-on-bone in my knee was a foggy memory. "Yep, you got it. On that trip, she was already with him, already halfway out the door."

I didn't know how the "door" idiom would translate, but it didn't matter. Paolo was already talking in his usual, low murmur. I tried following the sentences, hoping to single out

Scott Gould

the verbs and subjects and figure out what he was saying. I heard the word *freddo* a few times, sprinkled among phrases that evaporated before I could decipher them. *Freddo.*

Silvia leaned toward me. Over her shoulder, I saw her fiancé smiling in the background, tonguing a cigarette. "My father, he says that she seems cold the last time. Too cold. He says her cold makes sense now to him." Silvia was right. Paolo, too. Those were cold times.

So, I thought as I rearranged the jars and glasses on the table like a Three-Card Monty dealer, this isn't what I had planned. I didn't want melodrama, but I did want to create an effect. My desire was to tell stories and have the air in the room disappear for a moment. But they already knew somehow.

Freddo, Paolo said. Something was cold in Serra, years ago.

SESSANTAQUATTRO.

That first night I slept in a tiny room in a hotel down the mountain in Panicagliora, a village probably twice the size of Serra. Renza didn't offer to put me up for the night. I didn't blame her. I could tell by the look in her eyes that I was not unlike more scaffolding that would have to be erected then torn down before the wedding. It wasn't a mean look. I was, simply, in the way. So I drove to the hotel beside the pizza parlor.

The next morning, Paolo took me across the square to a squat, white stucco building with a huge wooden door. There were no hotels in Serra Pistoiese, no hostels, no quaint bed-and-breakfast places. But there was this place, the old ex-convent that, in the years since our first trip here, had been turned into small rental apartments, a building called Villa la Farfagliana. I began to worry about all the things in Serra that were exes. Paolo's ex-hotel, the ex-convent, ex-husbands limping around, asking questions in pig-Italian. The little village seemed to be evolving into a gathering spot for people and places that used to be something else.

With Paolo's help, I rented an apartment in the ex-convent for the length of my stay. It was small—just a kitchen and a little sitting room and a sleeping loft above that. A tight, spiral staircase led from the sitting room to the loft. The staircase was metal and shaky and creaked with every step. The shuttered windows in the kitchen and sitting room opened onto the deep valley below Serra and across to the low, worn mountains beyond. Logging had created odd, geometric patchworks of missing chestnut and syca-more trees that appeared lighter green on the slopes in the distance. The mountainside resembled a puzzle missing the last half dozen pieces.

Some sort of swallows—tiny slivers of birds that dive-bombed the air above the valley—spent the mornings and evenings feeding on insects I couldn't see. They were fearless flyers, banking and diving at strange, impossible angles. I threw open the heavy wooden kitchen shutters and poked my head into the open air, a good forty feet above the ground that fell away behind the building. Under me, a narrow terrace of houses balanced on the hillside. I could see tiny postage-stamp vegetable gardens and small patios full of children's toys and lawn chairs.

The swallows, usually one at a time, would gather speed fifty yards away from the window, then fly directly at my head, like dark bullets. I would see them coming and have time to brace myself and convince myself not to duck. *They have to veer, they have to dodge*, I whispered. At the last possible instant, I always ducked, turned my head and jerked back into the kitchen. The swallows came a couple feet from my face, close enough for me to see their eyes, then twisted instantly up the façade of the building. As I flinched, I saw the undersides of their wings, and I thought of Guilfoil, the gunner, riding in the tail of his B-17, banking blindly on the wind above Serra.

SESSANTACINQUE.

On the previous, awkward trip to Serra, my ex-wife did all of the talking. Her Italian was pretty good. (I imagine it still is.) But now, this trip, I needed a translator, one I wasn't married to. I'd contacted Antonluigi's sons earlier in the year to ask for their help. I didn't expect them to serve as translators—they were busy lawyers in Florence who spoke impeccable English—but I knew they could suggest someone. They never got back to me, uninterested, I suppose, that I was chasing down their father's story. I was surprised. But maybe they'd had enough of Guilfoil. I couldn't possibly conduct interviews by myself. When Paolo and his family (and I supposed, everyone else in Serra) began machine-gunning Italian, I would be clueless.

For a moment, I felt again like I did that first afternoon in Montecatini Terme—lost but not panicked, sure the right path would open up. And it did. The first full day in Serra, I walked into the lobby of the Farfagliana, and Paolo stood there with two men he introduced as Franco and Francesco, a father and son.

Franco, the father, was a thin, thin man who oozed energy and intensity. Something on him was always in motion—his hands or his eyebrows or the brown tooth that must have been false and *must* have had a home somewhere in his jaw, a tooth he worked around his mouth like a dark piece of hard candy. His voice was as thin as his body, compressed into a small escape of air that made him sound as though he were constantly on the verge of losing his breath.

Franco's son, Francesco, appeared as though he'd never

dipped a toe in his father's gene pool. His eyes, his dark skin tone, the way he stood, resembled his father in no way I could see. Francesco had a thoughtful, almost peaceful look on his face, and he seemed interested in my desire to find out more about Guilfoil's story. And he spoke English. Spoke it well, actually. His eyes flashed. I could tell he wanted to contribute to the story, be a part of it. Once Paolo explained, in Italian, why I was in Serra, Franco and Francesco immediately pointed to the road that led out of town, firing Italian phrases I couldn't follow. Paolo's eyebrows rose. I assumed he'd been taken by surprise.

Francesco looked at me and said in careful English, "Here is something for you." He leaned in. "Guilfoil is not the only man who fell to earth that day."

SESSANTASEI.

"There," Francesco said, translating for his father, "one of the flyers from the plane comes down here. Most eyes follow the plane. They hope it would not hit the houses. But some eyes follow this man. His parachute comes down there, in the chestnut tree. We use chestnut trees for everything. Even to save American flyers."

We were a few minutes down the mountain from Serra, in the direction of Panicagliora, where Francesco pulled onto the shoulder. Franco bolted from the car and waved toward the side of the road and began rattling off Italian, pointing to the air, then to the land just off the narrow road. We stood in the sun, and I felt the swelling and throbbing beginning under my kneecap. Francesco translated as best he could while his father fired phrases at him.

In the middle of the plot of land that bordered the road, a lone chestnut tree stood above the scrub shrubs and stalky weeds. Its branches spread in all directions. I had no problem imagining the tree reaching out and snagging a confused, terrified fighter pilot by his parachute strings.

Francesco continued to echo his father, trying to catch up with his descriptions of that day. He told me that several men from the village grabbed their rickety ladders—the ones they used for setting the olive tree nets—and cut the airman out of the chestnut. His leg was bleeding, so they carried him across the road to the Pensione Parenti.

Francesco pointed toward the other side of the road, at nothing in general. "The Pensione Parenti," he said, waving his arm as if he were formally introducing me to the building.

"*Dove?*" I asked. Where?

"There! Right there," he said. "That one."

The Pensione Parenti was hulking and abandoned, an ancient brick-and-stucco building directly across the road, with large wooden shutters beside the open windows and what looked to be nails protruding from the stucco. The sun beat down on us in the late afternoon; I had to shade my eyes to see the *pensione* clearly. The three of us sweated and mopped our brows. I wondered how long it had been since I'd popped a Lortab. But there, in the heat coming up from the cracked, unattended asphalt, I was suddenly chilled by the fact that I could see the tree where a scared man tangled in the branches and the abandoned hotel where he was carried by complete strangers who didn't speak his language.

Franco continued his story about the airman with a hurt leg. They took the American to an upper floor in the *pensione*, thinking he would be safer higher up. (I smiled at this: Mountain people thinking elevation equaled safety, even though it left them with a single escape route.) It didn't take long for the local Fascist contingent to drive up the mountain from Marliana, the nearest village with any size to it. They had seen the plane, too. They had, no doubt, counted parachutes in the sky.

Franco could not contain his disgust for the *Fascisti*, even after sixty some years. He told me how they came to the *pensione* and pushed by the female owner of the hotel, Argia Parenti, mounted the stairs and grabbed the American airman, forcing him to walk back downstairs on his bad leg. "They even kicked him in his wound," Franco said.

Nazi officers soon arrived and tried to question the airman, who refused to say anything more than the usual— name, rank, and serial number. His silence infuriated the Germans, Franco said, and they beat him in the lobby of the Pensione Parenti.

"We heard this all," Franco said. "It was hard to hear someone scream like that." Franco said that eventually the soldiers climbed back into their cars, taking the American with them.

I wanted a cinematic ending for this story, something

like: the American airman looked at the villagers as he was loaded into the Nazi car and winked or smiled confidently, silently thanking the people who cut him down. But Franco had no such conclusion. He ended his story simply, with a single bit of information. One of the local Fascists (one who kicked the airman, Franco thought) fled to South America after the war.

"I envy him his vacation," Franco said.

Sessantasette.

I asked Francesco and his father to stand in front of the old Pensione Parenti so I could take a picture of them. The sun had dropped behind the building. I wasn't sure there was enough light for a decent shot. I framed them with the *pensione* as a dark, looming backdrop. Francesco put his arm around his father. They still looked completely unrelated.

"Father," Francesco said in English, "smile big. We are part of history."

SESSANTOTTO.

They drove me back up the mountain to Serra, chatting the entire way in excited Italian about something. I liked to think it was about the pilot in the chestnut tree, but for all I knew, it could have been about the weather. As we entered Serra, Franco pointed at a man and began spewing Italian even faster. "Okay, okay," Francesco said, tapping on the horn. He told me over his shoulder, "That man is Giorgio Parenti. He knows about Guilfoil."

Giorgio was more than happy to be stopped in the street. It made him feel important. I could tell by the way he continually craned his head to see if the other villagers were watching. Francesco took it upon himself to explain everything to Giorgio. He pointed to the sky, then down the mountain toward Panicagliora, then at me. Giorgio possessed one of the largest heads I'd even seen, the size of a beach ball. When he finally talked, a huge, booming voice erupted from that big head of his.

The two men—Giorgio and Franco—were probably close to the same age. They began walking down a side street, one of the few in Serra, and Francesco motioned me to follow. "They are taking you to Guilfoil's grave," he whispered reverently.

My breath caught in my throat. I was suddenly excited, so excited I forgot about my knee and the grinding of the bones in my joint. I limped after them, trying to recall the original story Antonluigi had told me, about how Guilfoil was buried with a full religious ceremony in Serra's cemetery. But we had passed the cemetery on the way into town, a half mile in the opposite direction from where Giorgio and Franco scurried, walking faster than men their ages should.

In less than a minute, we came to a sloping road leading below the village, toward a public spring. I'd been down this road before, years ago, with Paolo and my ex-wife. People from Serra filled water bottles from the spring. I remembered drinking from it and noticing how tart the water was, like citrus had been magically added.

Franco stopped in front of an ancient car, which sat rusting on the side of the street. Gnarly volunteers, Italian versions of chickweed and ragweed, grew around wheel rims and through the crumbling quarter panels. Giorgio said something. Francesco asked him to repeat it.

"He says Guilfoil is buried under this car." Giorgio continued talking and Franco translated. "Yes, he is sure. Guilfoil's body is buried here."

"Under this car?" I asked, not believing my translator. "That's what he said?"

"Si," Francesco answered. "Here is Guilfoil."

"He's still here?"

"No, no," Francesco said. "My verbs are no good. He *was* here. For a while."

There was nothing magical about this place. Weeds and rusting metal, space that may at one time have been a garden, the back wall of a house without windows, a gravel two-rut road leading to a public spring. Antonluigi had told me of religion and incense and ceremony, of Guilfoil being lowered into a grave the villagers dug by themselves, about how Americans came later and exhumed his remains and took them to Chicago. I suddenly recalled how Antonluigi pronounced Chicago. *Chee-ka-goes.*

The two older men seemed proud they had brought me to the site of Guilfoil's burial. The look on their faces seemed to suggest my search was over. They had led me to the end of my story. I smiled at them and grabbed my camera. I photographed the car, and the two of them in front of it. They gazed beyond me and down the hill, into the chestnuts, standing like proud, successful explorers. I scribbled in my notebook.

They probably thought I was writing flowing, wonderful sentences about standing at the site of Guilfoil's grave in the dying afternoon light, at the foot of Serra, just where the village gave way to the forest. But instead, I wrote simply:

They are wrong.

This is not how Guilfoil ended, not where he ended.

This part of the story is a lie.

But this has been a good day.

SESSANTANOVE.

Most mornings, I ate a leftover roll from the café and took a few swigs of Coke from the liter bottle I kept in the small fridge, so I could have my first Lortab of the day. I didn't want it to bounce into an empty stomach. I opened the window to the mountains, watched the swallows as they darted and gyred, hunting for the invisible columns of warm air rising from the valley floor. I studied them, waiting for the Lortab to take the edge off the knife in my knee, and I thought about Guilfoil. The swallows zipped toward my open window, curious, and I wrote things down in my little notebook, ideas I would need for the Surdna people. Some of them were the truths I already knew, some were lies:

> *What is Guilfoil thinking?*
> *He makes lazy, buzzard-like circles above the village, low enough the people standing in the street and under the chestnut trees around the square can watch the tail of smoke that seems to be chasing the plane through the sky. Maybe Guilfoil feels the B-17 banking slightly, making its way clockwise around the top of the mountain. The sound is different now. That's no surprise. The engines are off and only the rush of wind over metal is audible inside his place in the turret. The flak-staccatos have stopped as well. Guilfoil is gliding as silently as possible, dying as quietly as he can.*
> *(Does he know that he is alone now, that the other nine – his nine friends – bailed out over the mountains? Guilfoil cannot see. He tried to tell them through the intercom*

when the plane was bucking and lurching at its worst. "A hole," he told anyone listening. "I think there is a hole in my head. I can't see a thing." Guilfoil doesn't remember that one of the crew members, one that could leave his weapon, crawled into the tail and saw the wound in Guilfoil's bare head and saw that Guilfoil had no sight, then turned away. He knew parachuting would not help Guilfoil. He wouldn't survive the fall. No one could bring themselves to answer Guilfoil on the intercom. He just heard hissing through his headphones.)

So. What does a man think when he glides to the end, the scream of the engines disappeared, the sounds of his friends no longer punching into his ears, everything replaced by the slipstream of air over the huge wings of the bomber, a sound that is almost a welcome quiet compared to the thrum that had hammered Guilfoil's ears all the way from Tunisia to Bologna?

Bologna. That is where the trouble begins. The flak is heavier than Guilfoil anticipates, than any of them have reason to expect. From his position in the tail, his eyes on the patchwork of farmland and railroads and highways below him, Guilfoil is constantly looking backward, in the direction they have already come. The flak pop like bottle rockets in the air around him. They are supposed to destroy the rail yards in Bologna. Create confusion. Twist some track. Mess things up.

Before the flak, there are jokes on the intercom about bombing Bologna, the kind of humor scared men create to forget about their fears. Over the water, from Tunisia past Sardinia, then to the west coast of Italy, there is running commentary about mustard with Bologna. About fried Bologna sandwiches. About Bologna and Swiss. Anything to make people laugh before the flak starts.

They release their bombs on Bologna. Guilfoil watches them waver in the air pockets on the way down, fighting gravity as they hurtle toward the ground. They hit the grid of city blocks, and soon the rail yards are blanketed with smoke. The flak splatters around them until one of the bottle rockets hits their plane. The Rhomar II.

Number 907. It has a hole in it now, and the air makes new sounds inside the plane, especially as the speed slows. The rest of the planes in the formation leave the Rhomar to fend for itself. Soon, as the Rhomar loses altitude, the German Messerschmitts arrive from below, like expected pests, and put more holes in 907. Time stops or moves too fast – Guilfoil can't decide which. He can't see. He can talk, but he can't see. He can hear. The sounds are changing. Engines are laboring, then feathering into silence. He can smell, too. The stink of burning oil and smoke. Guilfoil pulls the trigger on his machine gun, but he can't tell if he's actually firing.

Then suddenly, almost instantly it seems, Guilfoil senses he is alone, held aloft by Bernoulli's principle of moving air over a curved surface, causing magical lift. Guilfoil is being lifted, but gravity will eventually win. It always does in the end, brings everything down to earth one way or another.

(Flyers respect gravity because they defy it daily. They don't like to tempt it or make it mad. Thirty tons of metal isn't supposed to climb into the air and rise above the horizon, not supposed to fly hours and hours and turn rail yards into Pickup Stix.)

Guilfoil probably doesn't know the mountains below him—the ones surrounding Serra Pistoiese—are old, crotchety mountains worn by time and water and wind. They are round-topped, without peaks, without drama, covered with chestnut trees and poplars. The chestnuts cling to the last of their leaves, the ones still shimmering in the breezes that will carry snow and winter in a few weeks. Even though it is October, the chestnuts still give off a sticky, sweet smell.

Guilfoil can no longer see, but Serra watches him. The people follow his plane as it burns circles in the sky. What is Guilfoil thinking when he hears the B-17's wings clip the tops of the tallest chestnuts? Can he still hear then? Has the renegade flak that separated him from his skull finally taken away all of his senses? Does he feel gravity winning? Who knows any of this?

These days, we only imagine.

SETTANTA.

One morning, early in my first week, Silvia walked me to the café and under the shade, introduced me to Daniele and Luca, two young men who lived in Florence, but had, since they were kids, spent their summers in Serra. Serra was a very old village by personality; no one young stayed around long. Most of the young people moved an hour east to Florence, or west toward the coast, maybe to Lucca. Daniele and Luca still had family in the village, and to escape the thick, stagnant summer air in Florence, they spent their weekends in the mountains.

Daniele was dark-haired, with a round, soft face and a quick smile that burst across it easily. He was in the process of cultivating a respectable beer belly that he sucked in anytime a pretty girl walked by. When I looked at Daniele, I could tell instantly and exactly what he looked like twenty years earlier, when he was in the first grade. His looks would never change. Only the width of them would.

His friend, Luca, was more intense, with a scruffy dissident's beard and glasses like Paolo's that changed color in the sunlight. Luca was small and nervous, always glancing around as if someone were sneaking up on him. They had been friends since childhood, and had known Silvia for years. My guess was that everyone in that age bracket in Serra—the late twenties—knew everyone else, that they hung together for lack of anything to do when they met up in the mountains. I couldn't see them spending their days playing cards and telling stories in front of the café. There must have been other things to do that were out of sight, underground maybe, where I couldn't see them.

I liked Daniele and Luca the second I shook hands with them. The chemistry between the two of them was infectious. More importantly, they both spoke English very well. For days, I'd worried about finding a translator. Now, I had two. And both of them seemed genuinely excited about taking me around to talk with people. "I can practice my English," Daniele said.

I offered to pay them both, and Daniele laughed. Luca said if I bought Daniele beer, he would work all day long. Daniele ignored him, and I remember thinking they must be the kinds of friends who knew how to kid one another.

Daniele and Luca had heard of Guilfoil and the plane. Daniele pointed over his shoulder. "It crashed down the hill. We call that place *selva dell'apparecchio*, the little forest of the airplane."

Luca corrected him. "Little forest of the machine. But the only machine that has crashed here is an airplane, so people use that English word incorrectly."

Daniele said, "Big fucking deal. Did I use that correctly?" and he smiled at his ability to cuss in another tongue.

They said they would take me into the trees one morning, if I wanted to see where the plane went down. I started to ask them how far of a walk it was, but didn't want to come across like a foreign wimp. I mentally tallied the Lortabs I had remaining in the bottle. I would have to double-dose if I went down the path to the little forest of the airplane-machine.

SETTANTUNO.

Daniele and Luca were available to translate only on weekends. They had jobs in Florence during the week. So that first Saturday morning, they took me back down the mountain to the little town with the pizza place, Panicagliora, to meet Mario Mucchi. Mario owned an ice cream parlor on the edge of town, a tiny place that wouldn't really qualify as a gelateria. As we pulled up, Daniele told me ice cream stores in Italy were tax havens, a way to squirrel money away from the government. "That's why you see so much ice cream in Italy," he said. "And fat ice cream store owners."

Mario was indeed large, squeezed into a tight, stained tank-top. He sat with us under an umbrella just outside his store. Through a row of randomly planted teeth, he told me how, when he was thirteen, he watched parachutes drift from the sky while the plane circled and eventually went down near Serra. "While men were in the air, floating in the air," he said, "German airplanes shot at them. Like shooting birds that cannot fly good." I thought of the swallows outside my window.

Mario elaborated on the story of the man in the tree. "When they came to cut him down, he showed us the cross on his neck," he said. "Maybe he wanted us to know he was Christian. Maybe he thought he was going to die."

Without realizing it, he had corroborated the story I heard from Franco, about how the Fascists and Nazis took custody of the flyer and tortured him, trying to force him to talk. But Mario seemed bored by his story, as if he felt it was old news now.

He said that one time, a German command post was headquartered in the building right next door to his little ice cream store. Even this bit of information seemed like a yawn to Mario. However, his eyes lit up when he said he could tell me the four things he remembered most from the war. "The big four!" he hollered.

I looked back and forth from Daniele to Mario, waiting for this revelation to unfold, one I knew would include drama and body parts and blood. But Mario's forever-embedded recollections of the war—from a time when men dropped from the sky and hung in trees—were these: chicken stored in cans of jelly, chewing gum, chocolate bars, and bread shaped into a loaf and sliced.

"These things I had never dreamed of," Mario said, his eyes glazing a bit. "Bread cut before you must cut it. Miracle."

Luca leaned over to me. "Everyone was very poor, I hear," he whispered.

So maybe poverty dulled the drama of Nazis beating an airman who balanced on a bullet-riddled leg. In Mario's narrative of the war, chicken-in-gelatin ranked higher than parachute silk decorating a chestnut tree in town.

A woman called from inside the store. Daniele told me it was Delfa, Mario's wife. "She wants him to get back to work. Hold on," he said and ducked inside, reappearing with a perspiring white-haired woman wearing an apron stained with chocolate and fruit. She spit some Italian at Mario and he rolled his eyes. We had talked long enough for the sun to shift in the sky. It blazed behind Mario now, back-lighting him. I had to squint to see his face.

Luca asked Delfa if she remembered anything about the plane crashing in Serra, and Delfa cocked her head a little toward the road, as if she were trying to hear the memories instead of dredging them up.

"John," she said to Luca. "That's the one I remember. John."

Daniele nodded at her to continue, and Delfa launched into a long, intricate story of John, the British pilot. Delfa was ten years old when her family hid John in their house. (How he got there, she didn't recall. She just knew that one day, he was suddenly *there*.) John somehow developed a relationship with a local girl who brought him food, "and maybe other things," Daniele added, in Italian, raising his eyebrows. Delfa tossed her head at him.

The girlfriend's brother, according to Delfa, gave the British pilot a gun "for his protection." One day, the Brit was showing his girlfriend how to shoot the pistol and it went off in his hand. Unfortunately, the girlfriend happened to be looking a bit too carefully, and the bullet struck her in the head, and in Delfa's words "killed her deadly."

The British soldier fled to a town near Montecatini called Buggiano, where he was sheltered in a convent for a few days, after which he went to stay with another family in Montecatini. In that family, there was a young woman named Sorana. (The British pilot seemed to have little trouble attracting woman who wanted to care for him.) The Brit only stayed in Sorana's house for three or four days, when the Americans rolled through and liberated the area. They gave Sorana money for helping hide the pilot, enough money that "it changed her life," Delfa said. "Other people here in Panacagliora were jealous that she got money and all we had was a dead girl and a bad gun. My family was very mad at the Americans."

Delfa grunted toward Mario when she finished her story, and the two of them disappeared inside their store.

"Is good story, si?" Luca asked, and I nodded enthusiastically.

I was hearing tales that tap danced around the story of Guilfoil and the downed plane. I was learning that the memories people stored—whether about jellied chicken or dead girlfriends—belonged wholly to them. They catalogued them how they pleased. I was beginning to think that Antonluigi's story of Guilfoil might be suffering from the same (perhaps misguided) enthusiasm. Guilfoil coming to earth was the story for which Antonluigi carried the flame. It would never die as long as he kept telling it. And if he could find someone like me to write it down, so much the better, especially after he was gone. I limped down the steps into the street, a little privileged, but a bit let down for some reason.

Guilfoil was, when you got right down to it, just another story, no more, no less. And I always thought he might be more. I had hopes for him.

SETTANTADUE.

Mornings, if I wasn't out interviewing someone who knew something about Guilfoil and the crash, I would write in my notebook until I got hungry, then limp my way to the only store in Serra to buy lunch. The place sold fresh rolls, cheese and a variety of meats, depending on what the delivery truck had carted up the mountain.

The tight shelves of the small store were stocked randomly—canned goods next to boxes of cereal next to laundry soap, and the always-open door was the only way for light to filter into the store, bathing it in a shadowy glow that made it hard to read labels and prices on the items. The woman who heaved open the large metal, roll-up security door early each morning was brown-eyed and wary of me. She made me work for my order daily, claiming with her hands and her frowns that she didn't understand a word of English. I knew enough Italian to ask her name. Sonia.

After I ordered, paid and thanked Sonia (which seemed odd—thanking her for the language gauntlet she forced me to run), I heard her chuckling with her friend who'd witnessed the entire scenario. I knew they were laughing at me. I probably was funny: a man who staggered on one good leg and couldn't order the makings for lunch.

Back in my apartment, I put together a sandwich and swallowed a pair of Lortabs for dessert. I waited for the pills to land and watched the air show of swallows outside the window. Even in the middle of the day, in the heat, they found a reason to fly outside my window. The longer I sat, the better I could follow their movements. I tried to focus

Scott Gould

on a single bird and see if there was a pattern to his manic flight. I could never maintain my sights on him. When he looped into a group of other swallows, I lost him.

I didn't know why I thought of the swallows as males, until one lunchtime it struck me. I thought of them all as Guilfoil.

They were all dipping and diving toward Serra, toward the trees. The difference was, each of them made it back into the air alive, all pulled out of their dive toward the hills, all continued to circle, to live. But for me—especially when the Lortab struck—they became tiny Guilfoils, playing in the air above Serra, toying with gravity. The longer I watched, the slower they moved, until finally, before I laid down for a nap, they became still frames in the sky and I could see their eyes, and I realized they knew Guilfoil's story too. They had flown with him that day.

This feeling never lasted long. But I came to need it.

SETTANTATRÉ.

I had no concrete strategy for my revenge, which was short-sighted. I thought that once I performed my little condiment show for Paolo and Renza, they would beg for more information, more dirt about the breakup and divorce. I wanted the chance to tell them about the U-Haul debacle and the Clint Eastwood movie and—if I could ever figure out how to weave it in—the pierced penis. When I wasn't gathering Guilfoil interviews, I was sure I could entertain them about sitting under my pergola and drinking beer and listening to the wrens flutter in the Crossvine.

Then again, maybe I had a plan after all, and it depended on the stories I could bring myself to tell. There was a flaw in my strategy, though. It soon became apparent that Paolo did not want to hear stories. Neither did Renza. As if Paolo's pronouncement of *freddo* was all that needed to be said about her.

Each day, I found Paolo on the bench in front of his house or at the café, and I would try to wedge her into the conversation.

"I've been sad since she left," I would say.

He would answer: "We should go on a walk. That will make you happy."

And the two of us would hike down the mountain toward the spring or behind the village on the road that led to Paolo's garden. If my dosage had been a little off, I would hear my knee joint grinding against itself and I would limp and weave like a drunkard. If I was fully stoned, I floated above the cobblestones, drifting behind Paolo's careful steps, and the only pain was the dull, insistent ache of failure once again, and once again it was her fault.

Settantaquattro.

I loved dreaming on Lortab. I never realized the drug had such an effect during sleep. Maybe it wasn't on dreams generally, just mine.

All the little movies that ran through my head while I slept suddenly became intensely colored, the reds and yellows and blues blasting through the insane story lines. My dreams turned Technicolor. I looked forward to downing a pill after I brushed my teeth at night. I was always tired then, my knee filled with floating needles from the walking I'd done that day. I would crawl up my noisy, narrow spiral staircase and lay down and wait for the show when I closed my eyes. I was beginning to like Lortab too much.

I dreamed about her sometimes, about my ex-wife. I dreamed she was there in Serra with me. The stucco on Paolo's house was suddenly lime green and the café on the little non-square glowed from its windows. Always, she appeared only for a few minutes, as though she were checking on me.

I dreamed about my girls, too. The setting for these was back home, but home had turned strange colors as well. The pergola shimmered in orange. The clothes the girls wore in the dreams radiated like they were toxic.

In the morning, the bells on the church clanged and jarred the colors away. I wanted to stay asleep and keep the hyper-colors a little longer. When I limped down the spiral staircase and spread the shutters on the apartment's only window, I looked down and noticed how brown Serra was. The buildings, the rooftops, the streets—all a palette of earthy orange-ish, brown tones. It wasn't sad to see Serra this way; it just wasn't the color of my dreams.

SETTANTACINQUE.

The Italian Bank Teller wore a white denim skirt with courageous seams that barely held their own. When she bent to gather some Euros, I became woozy as my imagination kicked into a new gear. Silvia stood beside me, interpreting. I knew enough Italian to be an embarrassment in public, and Silvia helped me with essentials: directions, rent negotiations. And currency exchanges with a deep-eyed bank teller wearing a skirt the size of a chamois cloth.

Silvia was acquainted with the teller; she explained they had worked at the same company a couple of years ago. I was so focused on the skirt, I had not noticed the IBT was wearing a Pink Panther t-shirt. Seriously. The Pink Panther was depicted in, obviously, pink sequins. The size of her chest gave the Panther an odd 3-D effect. I stood there staring, silent, holding out my American dollars like an offering for the collection plate while the Pink Panther mocked me.

Silvia told her friend I was visiting from the United States. She told her I was a *scrittore*, a writer. This, I thought, would be impressive to the IBT. The Panther would pitch and heave at the thought of a foreign writer staying in the hills just above the bank. But the IBT didn't even look up from the form she filled out. The Panther was uncomfortably still, not a sequin stirring.

"He is writing about Serra," Silvia said.

The IBT took the bills from my hand, licked her thumb quickly, and began dealing the money on the counter in front of her into two piles. Silvia smiled at me. I tried to tell her telepathically that she was doing fine with the translation, but could she ramp up the introduction meter a bit and ask the IBT to join us all for dinner in Serra? Join us for anything. *Help me get my foot in the door, Silvia!* I pleaded with my eyes.

"No," the IBT said. "No."

For a split second, I thought she had turned down my silent invitation, when in fact, she tapped on a stack of bills and began shot gunning Italian at Silvia. They talked back and forth for a few seconds.

Silvia translated. "She tells you she cannot take the new money. Only the old money."

By new money, she meant the relatively new ten and twenty dollar bills with the enlarged pictures of Hamilton and Jackson, the images with a hint of color other than green.

"But it's good. It's cash," I said. "It's American." The IBT glared at me like I was a counterfeiter on parole. I don't think she appreciated me invoking my country. "It's fresh," I said. *Fresh.* Nice word, scrittore.

"No," the IBT hissed and slid the new money back toward me. Her eyes were brown as leather and they were telling me to take it or leave it. I nodded and she turned to count out a few Euros. Silvia shrugged her shoulders. "Sorry," she said. I shrugged back, the international sign for *What the fuck?*

The IBT was really truly beautiful. I thought about bank tellers back home, in their corporate conservative clothes— except of course on casual Friday when they go all crazy with a sweatshirt or jeans. It was difficult to tell how old she was. Depending on the tilt of her head, she could be thirty-five or twenty. Her unknown age gave her enough mystery to overcome the fact she was wearing Pink Panther sequins. And she had rejected my perfectly good, legal tender. But I didn't care. I watched the seams on the skirt. They smiled at me.

She handed me my Euros and fired off some new Italian at Silvia. I thought I heard one or two words I recognized. Silvia turned to me.

"Lorenza wants to know why you write about Serra. There

is nothing good about Serra, she say to you." The teller was
one of those, I thought. One of those people who hated everything: where she lived, where she worked, etc., etc.

I wanted to tell Lorenza that it was a long story, that
it involved a fighter pilot and a crash and a divorce and
sandals in Florence, but I just smiled and turned away. I
could tell Lorenza wasn't in the mood. All of the sudden,
neither was I.

SETTANTASEI.

One afternoon, when I was tired of following the manic swallows and fighting the pain in my knee, I sat at the tiny desk in my apartment and the image of Dr. Morton popped into my head. I had not thought of him in years, decades even. He was chairman of the English department that employed me while I was still a graduate student. It was a nice gesture by Wofford College, my alma mater. By filling in for a semester while a tenured professor took a sabbatical, the school gave English department alums attending graduate school the opportunity to get a teaching gig on their resumes before hitting the real job market. My friend Jim and I were the two grad students they brought in to teach the grunt courses that semester. Jim was a brooding poet with a dark beard. Once, he'd ridden a bus from Eugene, Oregon to Spartanburg, SC, and that biographical tidbit made him somewhat of an anomaly among the English faculty at the college. Most of them had never moved that far or that fast.

Dr. Morton fit into the seriously sedimentary category. He was a white-haired, nicotine-stained man. His fingers were the color of jaundice, his white mustache tinged on the edges like it had been dipped in curry powder. He saw himself as the Great Advisor because he was older and whiter than we were. Jim and I played basketball on Friday afternoons with students. That was our routine. Dr. Morton drank iced tea every morning at ten o'clock in the school's coffee house and held court for anyone who wanted to listen. That was his.

One day, Morton called me into his corner office in the Old Main building on campus. The air in his office was chalky with smoke. Near one window, a tall, elaborately scrolled desk stood at almost chest height. A stool sat in front of it. Several ashtrays littered the desk, full of cigarette butts. He noticed me notice the desk.

"Hemingway wrote standing up, too," he said when I walked in, as if he and Hemingway were members of the same furniture club.

He motioned to me to sit down in a low, soft chair. The room smelled of old smoke and old men. He asked how classes were going. How was I handling the grading? Was I getting out some and enjoying myself? He might have used the phrase *wild oats*. "So you want to write," he finally asked, but it sounded more like a statement. I nodded.

"I truly feel you should go to law school," he said, pulling a pipe from a stretched pocket on his cardigan. So, he smoked a pipe too. He sucked on it even though it was empty of any tobacco. The sound was like the opening and closing of a carburetor valve. I didn't know what to say. I didn't want to go to law school. I didn't like lawyers. They wore too many clothes and most of the ones I'd met were Republicans.

"Why's that?" I answered.

"You've had nothing happen to you. You have nothing to write about," he said, punctuating his sentences with airy sucks on his empty pipe. "Take Jimmy for instance."

Okay, I thought. I haven't ridden a Greyhound across the country, but there was time. Greyhound wasn't going out of business.

"He's got his dad," Dr. Morton said.

"I've got a father," I answered quickly, without thinking. I was confused by the discussion. *I'd never be a good lawyer*, I thought. *I can't follow conversations*.

"Yes, but did your father commit suicide?"

Dr. Morton went on to tell me that because Jim had scar tissue from his personal tragedy, he'd be a better writer than I could ever hope to be. My only salvation was the law. I was twenty-five years old. Dr. Morton was old enough to have a yellow mustache. There were so many things I could have thrown out. Like the value of imagination. Or the ability to lie. Or tell a story. I didn't think to ask him about the fact that Jim's father's untimely death was just one story. What happens when Jim is done with all those suicide poems? And what about the future tragedy I might face, like the crash-and-burn of a marriage?

I was too young to do battle with Dr. Morton on an intellectual or rational level. I could only get pissed. I wanted to punch him, but I wondered if the mustache gave him an unfair advantage. Extra padding on the lip. When you are twenty-five, you punch your way out of arguments. He told me I couldn't do what I'd planned to do. He was the kindergarten teacher taking away my toys.

I wanted to hit him, but I wanted to keep my job. I relaxed my fingers on my thighs. Even from my seat far below his desk, I could see leaves falling outside the window panes. It had been a bright, wet fall. The leaves had hung on as long as they could. Today, a breeze cleaned the trees. The leaves floating outside calmed me down.

"Just one man's opinion," he said. He propped on his stool. On his desk, I could see manuscripts. Not student work, but his own writing. I couldn't tell if the pages were fiction or academic essays, but they were ready to be mailed out for publication.

I told Dr. Morton I would think about it, and I did finally, on a day years and years later, in Italy, while I sat at a little desk, writing and watching swallows defy gravity. I thought, *You sorry fuck.*

Now, I had stories because I lost something. I lost a wife. I cried for days, and now I had a dark space where something used to be. Maybe a little like Jim the poet. I had Guilfoil, too. He died. I didn't know him, but he lost his brain in his turret and crashed to earth. So did all those other men.

I had stories about falling.

SETTANTASETTE.

B ad teachers will tell you to write what you know. Good ones will tell you to write what you know well enough to lie about:

Franco's father tells him not to look up, so he does. In the chestnut tree, the largest one in their front yard that sweeps toward the dirt, a man dangles from tiny strings like an escaped puppet. The man's head rolls back and forth on his shoulders, as if it trying to separate from his body, Franco thinks. His father smacks him on the head and says he told him not to look up. Franco wishes he had the courage to spit on his father's shoes.

The neighbors gather to watch the man twist in the branches. His pants legs are wet like he's pissed himself. The neighbors have already heard about the plane that crashed farther up the mountain, near Serra Pistoise. This is one of the men who jumped from the plane and floated down to the valley after the Messerschmitt fired among them. The man in the tree moves his arm suddenly in a weak wave, and the people duck like something's being thrown at them. He is only a few feet above their heads. Something dark drips from the toe of his boot. Franco's father says they use chestnut trees for everything—it's no wonder chestnuts save Americans as well.

Franco's father walks quickly to the shed beside their house and grabs the ladder he uses to gather honey from hives high in the branches. Another man trots across the street for rope. They loop the rope over a branch, then around the man's shoulders. Franco wonders briefly if they are going to hang him. Once, for only a second, the man opens his eyes and looks at them and smiles. They cut his strings with a hand scythe and lower him to the ground. Franco thinks he will probably be dead by the time he touches the dirt. Death doesn't bother Franco. He has imagined what the dead look like many times. Every time his father hits him in the temple.

The man's legs have tiny holes in them. His pants are heavy with blood. They load him on a cart and push him across the street to the Pensione Parenti, the only hotel in Panicagliora. Franco isn't surprised. Everything in town ends up, eventually, in Pensione Parenti. People get married there, drink themselves stupid there, die there. Babies have been born in Pensione Parenti. There is no reason a bleeding American flyer shouldn't be brought through the thick doors.

Franco isn't allowed beyond the threshold. His father thumps him on the skull and tells him to go home, so Franco doesn't. He balances on a bolt of chestnut logs beneath the side window, peering inside the main room of the pensione. Franco's father and another man prop the flyer in a straight-backed chair and hold him upright. Franco's uncle uses the hand scythe to cut away the flyer's pants, and Franco's father grimaces at the bullet holes. From where he spies on them, Franco thinks the holes look like dirty coins on the flyer's white, white skin. A woman, a Parenti, dabs at the holes with a wet rag, and the flyer snaps to life because of his pain. His eyes flash from face to face to face, and the Parenti woman pats him on the shoulder and asks the only English question she knows. Cigarette, Seniore?

Franco hears cars pull up in the front of the pensione. He has time to warn the people inside, so he doesn't. Normally, cars are reasons to be afraid. Only the powerful have cars on the mountainsides. Franco peeks around the corner of the building. Three cars idle in the pebble drive in front of the pensione. More men than seem to fit in the seats tumble from the open doors. Fascists and Germans, all of them clutching the stocks of rifles or grips of pistols. Their shoes click porch stones like tap dancers.

Franco watches. His father and the others step back from the flyer's chair as if they are revealing a new statue. The Germans smile. One of the Fascists shoves Franco's father, and the look on his father's face says, I know you now and I knew you before the war. I know where you live and I will kill you one day when I can get away with it.

Franco wishes his father would smack the Fascist on the temple.

One of the German soldiers throws a basin of water into the flyer's face, reviving him. He fires questions at the American in languages Franco doesn't know.

The Fascists herd the people out of the room before the beatings begin. Franco, for a moment, thinks he might be able to stay at the window and watch, but his father comes around the corner and grabs him by the hair, pulls him off the piece of wood. His father has a strange, new look on his face. Franco realizes his father has known all along he was watching. He wanted his son to see, to learn. He backhands Franco in one ear, and they walk across the road.

Under the tree, the men roll cigarettes. They pick specks of tobacco off their tongues. The torn pieces of parachute above them snap in the breeze. From the pensione, they hear the flyer scream and stop, scream and stop.

Franco's father tells him not to listen, so he does.

SETTANTOTTO.

One night at Il Poggiolino, I hatched my plan to have sex in Italy. I was a regular at Il Poggiolino, one of the few restaurants in Panicagliora. Late evenings just before dark, I would make the ten-minute trip down the mountain. They always sat me at table seven, and I thought it was kind of cool, giving me the same table every time I came in. Then again, they might have been making fun of me. Maybe table seven was the Limping Tourist Table, an inside joke. But number seven had a clear view of the television, though, and a decent angle on the large brick oven. Which is why I fell in love with the woman who slid the pizzas in and out of the fire.

Her dark hair was tied back with what looked to be a strip of bandana. She wore a t-shirt that was a size too small. What truly fascinated me and kept my eyes wandering from the television to the oven was the sheen of perspiration coating her body. Her face and neck and arms glowed constantly as she fed the fire. The couple of waitresses and the older man who drew draft beer for customers talked at her, but I never saw her speak. Never. She just nodded and rearranged her pizzas in the red glow of the oven.

Because of her, I always ordered pizza with prosciutto and mushroom. The waitress didn't add the prosciutto until The Glistening Woman slid the pizza from the oven, laying the meat on the cheese while it still bubbled. The Glistening Woman never touched the prosciutto or the pizza. Someone else decorated it. She only handled the paddle. She's found her niche, I thought.

That particular night, while I fueled the Lortab with more beer, this new plan seemed all too clear, as if a fog had lifted from a highway, and I could actually see the road. (That feeling was becoming all too familiar in Italy—the feeling of being lost, but being confident the right direction would open up.) Having sex in Italy would bring closure to...to something. I *sensed* closure was at hand, as near as The Glistening Pizza Cook.

I could find someone on my own terms while simultaneously thumbing my nose—and other related body parts—at my ex-wife. She would, of course, never know. But that would be okay. I'd know. The sly smile on my face wouldn't give me away.

SETTANTANOVE.

(Note to those who consider this plan the saddest, most misogynistic thing they've heard in years: Shut up. You don't know. You can't possibly fathom what it felt like to be in Italy with a woman who had already hatched an escape route into a future, one that didn't include you. There's something Freudian or Jungian or Einsteinian about wanting to fuck someone in the same country in which you got fucked over. It's ego or archetype or relativity. It would make me feel better, that much was for sure. And to this point, the only thing that made me feel better was Lortab, and it was a good buzz, but it wasn't enough. Maybe sex, no matter when or where it occurs, is *always* revenge for something, one way or the other. You don't know.)

OTTANTA.

And it wasn't the only plan I had concocted since my arrival. The other one involved saving a child in the village. I decided—no doubt under the influence of Lortab and *birra*—that the best way to win the favor of the village was to rescue one of their youngest members from near death. Perhaps snatch an infant from the fountain or pull a young girl from the path of a runaway Fiat. The problem was, I'd yet to see that many children roaming the streets, and the ones I did happen to spot weren't in any apparent danger. Serra wasn't exactly teeming with children; I would have better luck saving an octogenarian, but I was keeping my eyes open. I didn't want to miss my opportunity to be a hero in the village.

OTTANTUNO.

She would be one of my stories, I decided. I watched the pizza cook without trying to hide my stare. She was average height. Average weight. She was average, period. *Except*. Except that moist skin. I wondered what her skin felt like under that glow. I wondered if, when the evening was over and she was at home, if she sat near a fan, letting the slow rush of air evaporate the slickness on her skin. Her fingers must have been rough from handling the paddle for hours on end. She probably had a grip like a pipe fitter's.

My waitress, who could have been related to the perspiring pizza girl (they had the same eyes and a similar crooked smile), brought me my check. It didn't seem like she charged me enough, as if something had been left off the bill. I noticed she'd only charged me for two beers. I distinctly remembered having four. I had been drinking this brand called DAB. *Quattro media DABs*.

The waitress, who nodded to me the entire evening instead of speaking, finally asked me something, surprisingly in English. She gestured to the notebook I always carried with me. "What," she said, "you are writing?"

When you write in restaurants, people do one of two things. They assume you are writing about them and instantly avoid eye contact. Or they ask you what you're doing, maybe in an attempt to become a character on your page.

"Stories," I said. "Just stories."

She drew herself up, rehearsing in her head the next bit of English she would attempt. When she was ready, after a few awkward seconds, she told me her father wanted to know something: *Would I like to watch the World Cup match in*

the restaurant later in the week, after the restaurant closed?
I knew Italy would be playing Germany. "The kitchen will
be closed. We will lock doors. But we will serve you beer,"
she said, smiling. She was pretty, but she didn't glow like
the pizza cook.

I was being invited to a private event in a place I didn't
know a soul. I started to ask her if the pizza chef would be
there, but I knew that would be too forward, and perhaps
too hard to communicate in English. I suddenly remembered I hadn't gotten a good look at the pizza girl's hand. I
didn't know if there was a ring. Or maybe she didn't wear
one while she maneuvered pizzas in and out of the oven.

The waitress waited patiently for an answer. "*Quando?*" I
asked and she grinned.

"After you finish eating that night?" she answered. "You
will be here anyway, right? You are always here." She
laughed. I realized then that transparency was its own international language. She knew—and her father did, too—that
I'd be back again and again, every night, leering at the pizza
cook, drinking too much beer, fabricating Lortab strategies
to make myself feel better. They could see right through me,
and they invited me anyway.

I told the waitress to thank her father for me, and I would
see them soon.

"He thinks because you are blond, you are fan for
Germany," she said, giggling.

"No, no," I assured her. "*Italia!*" I said it loud enough for
the pizza cook to hear, but she didn't even turn away from
her oven.

OTTANTADUE.

My ex-wife was an obsessive list maker who couldn't sit still for long. Shark-like, she moved constantly to keep herself alive, I suppose, in a daily quest to mark things off her fistful of lists. I, on the other hand, was always perfectly content to sit and observe the world passing by, because there were always too many characters to watch. Or maybe I was just lazy.

So I was surprised that, after only a week in Serra, I found myself restlessly making a list of things I needed to gather up for a trip to the coast. I hadn't planned on any day trips. I figured they would involve walking, and I was trying to cut down on that. And I knew leaving Guilfoil Country just when I was beginning to feel comfortable interviewing eye-witnesses to the crash wasn't wise, but the sense of isolation was pressing down, even on my knee, which had reached (and maintained) the size of a decent cantaloupe and felt like someone was rubbing a rattail file back and forth in the joint. I needed the distraction of a new location.

I drove to Lido di Camaiore, a touristy resort town about forty-five minutes west of Lucca. It immediately reminded me of Myrtle Beach, back in South Carolina: pasty-skinned tourists sweating and crowding the sidewalks in front of souvenir shops and ice cream parlors; rows of umbrellas lining the narrow beach; cheap seafood restaurants with shiny, plastic outdoor tables baking in the sun.

I found a decent hotel, The Europa, at a good price, with a large pool and a small bar, and I laid down on the bed while the air conditioner whirred to life. I stared at the ceiling for ten minutes or so before I began to cry.

These weren't gut-wracking, lose-your-breath sobs. Just tears that leaked from the corners of my eyes. Part of it, I knew, was because I missed my children. Some of it, I had to confess, was because I missed my marriage. I'd taken over the role of list-maker and constant mover, and I didn't want the job. I wanted to be a bullet point on the list and perhaps part of the motion, but I was unprepared to take on the entire task. I couldn't see the ceiling anymore. Outside, I heard Italian women yelling at their children in the pool. The isolation I'd felt in Serra had only intensified on the coast. I thought about wasted Euros and lost time.

I was convinced I'd finished the sobbing stage years ago, when she first left. Back then, I spent days sitting in a dark room—ironically, the place she'd dubbed the *sunroom*, though it never received any direct sun—my eyes bloated and unfocused, waiting for something to dry them out, like evaporation or a change in the weather. Anything. But here was a new batch of tears. I wondered if Guilfoil cried when his plane was going down, if there was enough of a brain left in his young skull to register sadness and impending loss. From the pictures I'd seen of Guilfoil, I could tell he was the kind of boy who tried to avoid tears, probably tried to avoid emotion of any kind, except perhaps anger.

I decided, lying there within hearing-distance of the ocean and the Italian children scaring their mothers in the deep end of the pool, that I would make no more lists during this entire trip. And, when I returned to the Serra, if I wanted to sit all day in the frame of my apartment window and watch the swallows dogfight, I would. I gulped two Lortabs, put on a clean shirt and headed for the hotel bar.

The least I could do to help my mood was try to get laid. More revenge. Less crying.

OTTANTATRÉ.

Marco was The Europa's night-shift bartender, the resident expert on everything, who wasn't afraid to share his knowledge with anyone who bought a drink. He knew I was from New York before I spoke. He knew why I was in town. He knew Boston was only a short drive from Los Angeles. So really, Marco didn't know shit. But in the great—and I assume international—tradition of bartending, he could fake anything.

Mary sat on my right. A Brit, she was travel planner and group coordinator who had been on the coast for eleven weeks. She seemed proud of the number eleven. She owned a head of thin, flat hair the color of winter grass that lay matted against her skull as though she'd been sleeping for most of those eleven weeks. Her face was as plain as sand. Except for her mouth. She had a mouth that she stole from someone beautiful, round and perfect with two half-moons of loud, red lipstick hiding her teeth, teeth which were, antithetical to the British cliché, straight and white. Mary was probably in her late 50s, too old, I thought, to be planning travel for vacation-starved Brits and sitting in a hotel bar with Marco, the Answer Man.

She apologized immediately for her station in life. "I have to work," she said. "I've lost my pension." I asked her how that happened, and her eyes filled with tears. (More crying, I didn't need.) "It's gone," she said. "Just gone." I ordered another vodka tonic for six Euro. I never found out how Mary lost her pension; she dropped the subject as quickly as it had come up.

Mary was the wingman for Natalie, the slightly chubby girl two barstools down from me. Natalie was the loud Brit of the two. I could tell Marco and Natalie had something going on. They swapped private jokes across me and Mary, private looks that flashed now and then. Natalie was back for more. I could feel Natalie's thought process boring a hole in my head. If she could pawn Mary off on me by closing time, Marco would have a free run at her. Natalie leaned across her friend's chest to whisper to me. "Shame about Mary's pension, love. Bloody shame." Mary pouted her pretty mouth in my direction.

I have never been good in a bar. I end up listening to what I'm saying, and the things that come out of my mouth embarrass me. I regularly stumble over simple sentences. The women I've ended up with—ex-wife included—were the ones impressed with my listening skills. I struck them as unusually sensitive, when actually, I was simply avoiding my inability to carry on a conversation.

A replay of the Italy-Ukraine World Cup match beamed from the television behind Marco. A larger monitor in the adjacent room entertained a few dozen Italian and German tourists, most of whom sat on chairs they pilfered from the restaurant tables. Their occasional roars flowed into the bar like waves. Mary drank Coke after Coke from small glasses. Natalie drank whatever alcoholic concoction Marco put in front of her. Natalie's volume turned up louder to compete with the cheers from the other room. I was annihilated. The double-shot of Lortab had long made its way to my head, and the world spun into a suddenly wonderful place to be. I forgot all about staring at the ceiling and crying. Mary's mouth was instantly insanely sensuous, and Natalie's screeching evolved into a strange aria with British overtones.

I realized I was leering at Mary, but in my Lortab haze, I was convinced leering was exactly what she craved. *She probably hasn't had a good leer since she lost her pension.* I thought I should suggest she change conditioner for that hair of hers, use something to conjure up a bit more volume. I asked her if she could afford conditioner without a pension, and she gazed at me as if I'd said something crude about a body part. She must have thought I was making fun of her lack of a pension plan. Natalie kept using the word *party* over and over, lengthening its pronunciation. "Oh, we love to pahr-tay, don't we, Mary?" she would say. "We're looking to go to a pahr-tay later. Any kind of pahr-tay will do, love."

Marco smiled at me and poured me another vodka. "Free on me," he said. Another shot of their house-brand vodka would send me dangerously close to a coma. I looked at Mary.

"I have a pension," I said. Or meant to say. But I think I might have said that I had a penis. The pension part was a lie. I had half a pension, half of my retirement. My ex-wife had the other half. Mary didn't respond, so I repeated it, intent on correcting my lie.

"I have half a penis," I said, thinking I was still talking about retirement plans. But words meant nothing, suddenly. Penis and pension, Marco and Natalie, Mary Mary Quite Contrary. The soccer players on television were ants marching manically on a green field. Marco clucked his tongue at me and laughed, and before I could focus on the chair next to me, it was empty. Mary had fled, her thin hair no doubt flying, and Natalie was writing something on a napkin for Marco. Probably the location of a pahr-tay. He smiled at her.

I said, "*Andiamo?*" which means let's go, but I meant to ask if the two British travel planners had gone. Marco, ever the bartender, told me that, No, he had to stay, but I could go anywhere I liked. I tried to sneak a look at the napkin, but he folded it into a vest pocket. Italy scored a final goal, and the room emptied with loud, deep cheering.

I stumbled toward the pool, wondering whether I would be happier with a pension or a penis. Or half of either. I fell asleep on a lounge chair near the diving board and stayed there until a security guard woke me up sometime before dawn.

In the pool chair that night, I dreamt of Guilfoil. In my dreams, he was going down in flames, but he never seemed to hit the ground.

OTTANTAQUATTRO.

The next evening, back in my little apartment in Serra, I swallowed a Lortab and watched the flies dogfight in the airspace in the center of the room. I'd been studying the flies a lot lately. There seemed to be a main *mosca* tonight, an Alpha Fly around whom (or which?) the rest of the flies orbited. It was very Copernican. Or was it Ptolemaic? That was part of my problem. I knew half of a lot of shit. I knew it was either Ptolemy or Copernicus who decided we weren't the center of the universe, but I couldn't remember who the heretic was. I'm good at cocktail parties because I know a little about a lot. I can begin dozens of conversations I can't end, but people think I'm smart.

But I didn't feel so smart. I was no longer the center of any universe. I was out there revolving around something big, something with a shit ton of gravity that kept me locked in orbit.

The thin light from the open windows faded and I couldn't follow the flies in the twilight, but I could hear them in their last whines, then it struck me, not so much like the proverbial ton of bricks, but more like a tiny switch that clicked somewhere in the back of my head. I knew who I was now: I was Guilfoil.

We had both come to the same village on the mountainside, looking for a soft place to land. Both our brains were scrambled. We couldn't see straight. There was no longer pain, just resignation. And maybe we had some hope that the village would rescue us, keep us from the guns and the *cinghiale*.

Guilfoil was me decades before I knew him. I was Guilfoil now. And I didn't know whether to rejoice about the discovery or cry again. I fell asleep in the dark and woke up the next morning on the same couch, curled up like I was protecting myself, the flies disappeared, the swallows already banking and dive-bombing the air over the valley just outside the windows.

OTTANTACINQUE.

I was wearing a wristwatch I wasn't used to. It was a really nice one a friend gave me last spring. One of his company's vendors presented it to him, and he already had a number of wristwatches lined up in waiting, so he passed it along to me. According to the directions, it was supposed to set and reset itself continuously by picking up a satellite signal from somewhere in space. All I had to do, allegedly, was lay the watch on a windowsill in the evening, and the magical resetting would take place as I slept. Each night since I'd arrived in Serra, I carefully placed the watch in front of the open window, tilting the face toward the sky where the swallows played, so as to facilitate satellite hook-up. But the watch remained stubbornly locked in Eastern Standard, like it desperately missed that time zone and refused to abandon it.

OTTANTASEI.

I met Daniele and Luca at the benches in front of the café. The plan was to walk down the mountain to the site of the Rhomar's crash. They brought two friends with them, Simone and Claudio. In the large circle of shade below the single chestnut tree, they gathered like excited first graders, waiting for the field trip to start.

Claudio was an older man, probably in his sixties, but because he was wiry and nervous, he seemed younger. He resembled a thin Mel Brooks. When he couldn't figure out what to do with his hands, he lit a cigarette. The other new guy, Simone, was thick and powerful, his hair cut short, military style. Daniele told me Simone was a lumberjack. I didn't doubt it. He had a body like a guy who played linebacker in high school. And although much of his muscle had given way to softer tissue, I had no trouble imagining him wrestling logs off a mountainside.

We started toward the *selva dell'apparecchio*, and I felt the Lortab kick in. I'd taken two back in the apartment as a sort of substitute breakfast, and tucked an extra in my jeans pocket, just in case. My limp was getting worse, so bad in fact, I was scared I might start walking in painful circles, spinning on the only good leg.

Daniele and Simone led us down the road behind Serra. The cracked cement and asphalt gave way to dirt and occasional gravel. The incline was steep enough to bring me into a slide now and then. The road quickly evaporated into a two-rut path. The last time it had been damp—god knows when—a tractor of some kind had left deep tracks in the mud, which had hardened into dark-colored knobs that helped with the footing.

I wanted to scream. The worst thing for my knee was going down stairs, or in this case, down hills. The pressure from the added gravity felt like someone digging in my joint with a knitting needle, and the pain traveled up my back and exploded near the top of my head. I thought about the third Lortab nestled in my pocket, but decided to save it. I didn't dare complain. How do you whine to a sixty-year-old man who scrabbled over the rocks like a nicotine-fueled mountain goat? Or to an overweight lumberjack, for crissakes? Daniele huffed a little, but Luca was fine. I didn't want to be the soft American. I clamped my jaw so tightly my back teeth ached.

Daniele and Simone stopped at a fork in the narrow two-rut path and argued in loud Italian about which way to go. Daniele wanted right. Simone won with a left. I lifted the weight off my bad leg. Daniele looked at me. "Simone is a pig but pigs have a good sense of direction," he said in English, smiling. Simone had no idea of what his friend had said.

Under the canopy of chestnuts and pines—which grew thicker the farther we hiked—the air was steamy and thick. We were drenched in sweat. The shade was no help. It reminded me of hiking in the Appalachians in August, and for a moment, I was homesick.

As we neared the crash site, I expected, at any moment, to hear the hum of angels' voices, some sort of heavenly fanfare, expected to see some golden light off in the forest floor that signified holy ground—where a dead man came to earth and was rescued to a proper grave by a band of feisty villagers. When I wasn't watching my footing, I kept my eyes out for signs of the consecrated spot in the woods, for some signal that I had arrived at the sacred site where Guilfoil found the beginning of his long rest.

But the only thing that happened was Simone waved his beefy arm in the general direction of the chestnuts just off the road and said, *"Ecco qui."* Here it is.

Luca explained that Guilfoil's plane came down in this general area. "They say very few pieces of it broke off. It just—whamp!—landed here. There was no big fire for some reason. Just big noise."

The ground they motioned to was perhaps a bit more cleared then the other side of the road. The chestnuts didn't look any worse for wear, maybe a few younger, smaller ones and a couple of dead trunks lying in the briars, which were thick and biting.

Daniele said a few years ago, a man hunting mushrooms brought a metal detector to the site, but only discovered a few shards of steel. Claudio and Simone were impatient because they couldn't understand what Daniele told me, so he translated for them. Claudio's eyes lit up when heard a mention about pieces of the plane. Around his cigarette he told us that his grandmother had used a chunk of the plane's fuselage as a lid for her cook pot.

Daniele said that soon after the crash, a procession of villagers came to the crash site and *ripped* the plane. "I know this is the wrong word," he said, "but you maybe get what I mean, yes?"

Ripped was the perfect description for the dismantling of Guilfoil's plane. I already knew that the village was so poor during the war, they had to hone their resourcefulness just to survive. Ripping apart a plane that cooled under the chestnuts seemed like a justifiable act to them, I imagined.

The light at the crash site filtered in wavering yellow shafts through the chestnut and poplar limbs. Spring seed pods from the chestnuts littered the ground like an army of mini-porcupines under our feet. I looked at the legs of my jeans. They were dotted with the Italian equivalent of beggar's lice. The crash site was an apt memorial to Guilfoil. This was probably what it looked like before he came to earth, wild and overgrown.

Luca said he'd heard that villagers watched the plane circle Serra twice, using their prayers to keep the B-17 from hitting their village. Some of the witnesses said the plane was on fire. Some said it was only smoking. (The difference between the truth and the story—the difference between a fireball and a smoke signal.) I liked to imagine the chestnuts reached up from the mountainside and grabbed the Rhomar and pulled it to earth, gently, almost peacefully.

There was something disconcerting about standing in the place where a man died and fell to earth, even though there was no monument to the event. Then, I realized what was missing. *Sounds.* It was strangely quiet under the chestnuts, probably the same sort of silence that enveloped the villagers while they stared at the smoking plane. That morning, surrounded by Simone and Claudio and Luca and Daniele, it was quiet like church, and for the first time since dawn, I didn't feel my knee.

OTTANTASETTE.

I finally sat at the wicker card table outside the café, but not to play cards. I was there to speak with Roberto Parenti, a tiny little man who hid most of his face behind huge eyeglasses perched on his nub of a nose. Roberto was missing the index finger on his right hand, and the entire time we talked, he orchestrated the conversation with his abbreviated finger.

It was too early in the morning for the local card sharks. A breeze blew (thankfully) over the top of the mountain and whistled down Serra's main street. I thought it felt cooler, like we'd earned a break in the heat. I was more than happy to sit. My knee reminded me I'd forgotten to take any Lortab for breakfast.

Daniele introduced us and explained to Roberto why I was here. The look on Roberto's face told me he already knew who I was. By now, word had filtered through the village about the limping American and his notebooks and his questions. Roberto seemed rehearsed, as if he'd practiced telling his story. I didn't have to ask any questions; I just had to stay out of his way. Daniele put his hand up to stop Roberto, so he could translate the staccato Italian Roberto fired out. Roberto never took his eyes off me while Daniele translated.

Roberto was seventeen years old, on the edge of manhood, the year Guilfoil went down. When the plane crashed through the trees, fifteen of the men from the village (Roberto was very, very specific—punching the air with his fingerless finger and repeating *quindici* several times) hiked down the same two ruts I'd limped along yesterday. They followed the echoes of the noises the Rhomar made when it crashed—the snapping of chestnuts, the singing stress of air over the wings, the crunch of metal twisting in directions it shouldn't.

According to Roberto, the plane was still smoking when they arrived at the site, and some of the men were afraid the hot metal would somehow explode. Alvaro Parenti was afraid of nothing. He was the unofficial leader in the village, a big man with a big voice who never shrank from anything: Germans, Fascists, cooling metal of a fuselage.

Alvaro studied the plane for a moment from the outside. It had crashed on its belly and upon its entry into the trees the fuselage had cracked like a piñata, spilling contents on the forest floor—seats, boxes and extra parachutes. Tiny funnels of smoke drifted from the split belly of the plane. Alvaro eventually crawled through the opening.

"Then," Roberto said, "he called to us. He said he had found a man on fire." Some of the others climbed in after him, and when they reappeared, they gingerly carried a dead American flyer. Guilfoil.

"He was smoking," Roberto remembered. "I could smell his skin burning. He was so young. He looked no older than me. It was hard to see a teenager like me that way. Burning."

By the time the men laid Guilfoil at the base of a chestnut, the local *Fascisti* arrived in a beat up car that belched smoke of its own. The guns they carried stuck up like tree limbs. Alvaro stood between Guilfoil and the Fascist contingent, protecting the dead flyer, Roberto remembered.

The Fascists knew Alvaro was a respected man in the village. That, and his size, earned him some leeway with the men in the car. "They saw no fear on his face," Roberto said, stabbing with his half-finger. "The only people they could control were the scared ones."

There was a long, loud discussion that echoed beneath the trees. The Fascists wanted to search the body, then dump it in the woods for the wild boar, the *cinghiale*, to eat. Alvaro refused. He told them that the young man would be buried in their *cimitero*, by the priest. Roberto remembered Alvaro glaring at the men with the guns, telling them, "When a man dies, he has paid for all his sins, so he is no more your enemy."

The Fascists gave up. Short of drawing a gun on Alvaro, they were not going to get the body. They had enough trouble with the locals. They didn't need more. They maneuvered their car between the trees and retreated back up the hill.

"Someone went for a cart and horse," Roberto remembered. "The men loaded the body on the cart and took it up the hill. I didn't help them. I was too scared. The body was still smoking."

In Roberto's memory, the body never extinguished. He was haunted still by the sight of a teenager burning. He saw, in the instant Alvaro emerged from the plane, the possibility of what could happen to young men at war. Roberto was on the verge of conscription at that time, I guessed. Seventeen or so, when young men are immortal, bulletproof, but there, in front of his eyes, was a reminder that skulls can be shot away, that flesh can burn. For Roberto, the war will always be that single, dominating image: Guilfoil on fire.

And I wondered, sitting at the card table, listening to Roberto's story, how much of it was true. Could the body have really been on fire? Were his clothes truly smoking when Guilfoil was pulled from the Rhomar?

I was at it again, watching the *idea* of truth bump heads with the real truth of a story. But it didn't matter that morning. In my left ear, Daniele translated what Roberto said. He watched me receive the English version. He searched for my reaction. Behind the huge glasses on his round face, Roberto's eyes filled with tears. He prodded the air with his missing finger.

The truth makes you cry, I decided. Lies don't bring tears. In Roberto's mind, the burning teenager was gospel, and I believed every damn word of it.

OTTANTOTTO.

The B-17 disappears below the tree line, into the thick chestnut groves on the western slope of the mountains. More of a simple, sharp crack than a full-fledged explosion. No ball of fire in the sky, no plume of sudden smoke.

Roberto stands in the square, as close as he can get to Alvaro. Even though Roberto is on the razor's edge of becoming a man, he likes to feel safe, likes to see protection in front of him. And Alvaro will always protect him. A dozen or so men gather on the stones in the front of the negozio and leave minutes after the plane disappears, before the Fascists have a chance to arrive in their cars. Roberto walks in Alvaro's path, listening.

A half mile more and the smell of wood smoke and burnt gasoline strikes their noses. A quarter mile more and the thin road divides. They go left and find the tops of several chestnut trees lying in the road, trees the plane clipped as it entered the canopy of the forest. Another switchback and the plane rises in front of them, smoldering dragon-like in the crisscross of tree trunks and limbs and metal. Roberto hangs back, watching Alvaro approach the plane. Alvaro is the leader in Serra. If he does nothing, nothing will happen.

The fuselage of the plane is cracked like a bad eggshell. Alvaro puts his head in the hole. He retreats and walks to the rear, where the tail of the plane is askew like a broken limb. Alvaro peers in the shadows there, too, then announces that a man is inside, and he is more than likely dead.

Alvaro appoints a helper from the group, and they descend into the tail section of the plane. When they emerge, they are *dragging (as gently as they can) a man who is not much more than a boy, a flyer as young as Roberto, perhaps. Blood from his head has soaked the shoulders of his flight suit. What Roberto can't understand is why the boy-man is smoking.*

Little ribbons of smoke or vapor or fog rise from the flight suit. Alvaro's helper tries to keep his nose away from the smoke. He grimaces like a man who has tasted something rotten. Alvaro's expression doesn't alter. He cradles the flyer and folds him onto the ground, like a father putting down his child for a nap. The dead flyer continues to smoke. Roberto has seen dead pigeons and chickens in the barnyard below the village, but never a human, never something so large, something that occupies so much space. Something so much like him.

The men don't hear the group approach behind them, a mixture of local Fascist noisemakers, in their makeshift uniforms, and a pair of German officers. Roberto has not learned to tell ranks by the number of medals and stripes, but these two don't seem overly important.

The Fascists and the German duo talk directly to Alvaro. He is the ranking member of the village group. The smoke has gathered in the chestnut branches that remain above the plane, like a fog refusing to lift.

The German officers, in their broken Italian and quick hand movements, tell Alvaro they are going to strip the dead flyer and look for maps and papers, then leave him to rot in the woods. They are after information they can pass to those above them. They care more about papers than flesh.

Alvaro hitches his pants. He doesn't shift his gaze from the men in front of him. His face is calm, like a man just awakened from sleep. Alvaro is one of the tallest men in the village. He can look the Germans in the eye without tilting his head upward. Alvaro speaks to them in a very low, very slow voice. He wants everyone to hear without having to repeat himself. He tells them that this man, this boy—this son of somebody's father—will be buried in Serra, in the cemetery, in ground blessed by God. The Germans shake their heads. They say they will take care of the body as they see fit.

Alvaro takes a deep, long breath, expanding his chest,

breathing in the smoke that swirls around them. He speaks loudly now, too loud for the quiet of the chestnut grove. "When a man dies," Alvero says, "he has paid for all of his sins, so he is no more your enemy. We will bury him in Serra."

There is no more to say. The German officers have bigger problems than this. They turn smartly on their heels and disappear into the trees with their Fascist guides. The speed with which they move suggests they will be back, that the village hasn't heard the last of this.

Alvaro sends a pair of villagers back to Serra for a cart big enough to carry a body. The body finally stops smoking, and Roberto takes a few tentative steps toward it. Roberto wonders what the boy, Guilfoil, thought when he suddenly realized he would never see tomorrow.

That, Roberto imagines, would be the saddest second of someone's life.

OTTANTANOVE.

Lorenza left the bank around 5:30. I knew this because I was hiding behind the corner of a nearby building, watching her. I'd always enjoyed spying. (I think everybody does. I wonder if it's learned behavior or if there is a strand of DNA common to all humans that causes us to look when we know we shouldn't.) When I was a kid, I climbed a huge magnolia tree at the edge of the Adams' yard and spied on Cheryl Shuler and her Kingstree High School Boll Weevil cheerleading squad. When I was twelve, Billy Stackley and I used to lie on our stomachs in the overgrown azaleas and watch Bonnie Kraft in her upstairs window. But that wasn't really spying. She knew we were there.

With Lorenza, I was committed to an all-out strategy. I had time on my hands. I fortified myself with a Lortab and a couple of Moretti's and pulled a stakeout near the small branch bank where she worked. I saw Lorenza moving inside the glass. She wasn't sporting the Pink Panther shirt today. It looked more like a golf shirt of some kind, an Izod maybe, which gave me immediate hope. If, by some miracle, Lorenza played golf, I would have something to talk to her about. *Try* and talk to her about. I could do a lot of golf handsignals. The swing. Putting. Hand above the eyes watching a drive sail down the imaginary fairway.

The sun beat down on me in my hiding place. I hoped I'd have a chance to stop sweating before I approached Lorenza. I didn't want to be glowing from perspiration. The sun heated up the Lortab, I'm convinced, like some sort of crystal meth-like concoction. I tried to focus on the bank's front window, but the heat made me think about my previous trip to Italy, the egg-shell-and-evil-sandal trip. I'd stalked my ex-wife a bit back then, watching her to see if she revealed any new clues that would explain her need to flee. I'd followed her in the market in Florence while she fingered silk scarves or hung leather bags on her shoulder. I enjoyed watching her when she didn't realize it.

During that trip, I didn't know there was another man; I was only aware of my failure to hold things together. And while I spied in the market, she gave nothing away. Once she caught me staring from a few booths over. She seemed initially embarrassed, then maybe a bit angry that I was watching her. I felt entitled. She'd been my wife for seventeen years.

"Stop," she said. "You're not helping anything."

NOVANTA.

Lorenza exited the bank like a model, floating instead of actually taking steps, magically moving the air in front of her. Or maybe it was the Lortab playing with my focus.

Before I could gather myself and approach her, she moved toward a scooter and mounted it. An aqua-colored Vespa, the old-school model, not the modern kind of moped that resembles a shrunken crotch rocket. In a second, Lorenza zipped off.

I jumped into my rented VW, keeping her in sight. She headed down the main road out of Panicagliora, waving at a couple of cars going in the opposite direction. She hammered the throttle on the Vespa, taking curves with a lean. I loved her suddenly for her crazy speed.

She buzzed up a side road, not far from the Il Poggiolino. I had to wait for a couple of cyclists before I could make a left turn and continue slightly downhill after her. I quickly found myself in a residential area, a place where families lived, I realized. Children. Husbands. Witnesses. Lorenza didn't wear a wedding band at the bank. I knew that. I saw dads and their kids in the small yards. I couldn't find the ocean-colored Vespa. Lorenza had disappeared. I would have to ask Silvia for help. I still needed Lorenza, still wanted her. She was important to wherever the story went. But for now, the story stalled, with me lurking behind the slightly tinted windshield of my rental car, wishing the sun would set quickly and give me new places to hide.

Novantuno.

They told me we were going to see Adriana, and when they said *Adriana*, they whispered the word like an incantation. Adriana was not a year-round resident of Serra, Daniele said. "She spends the hot time of the year here. She lives in Rome, I think." Luca told me more of her story as we walked up the hill to Adriana's house. He said she spent all of her summers in Serra when she was a young girl. "And they say she was very beautiful. People talk still about the looks she carried with her."

Now, Adriana was in her eighties. She opened the door to her house, and I was still a little out of breath from the climb. And the knee—I dragged it up the hill like a piece of cordwood. She didn't give us much of a hello, just a smile that broke the lines in her face, then she led us through a narrow hallway to the balcony in the rear. Even in the cool, dark of the house, I could see the art: modern, original oil paintings and ceramic wall hangings; a small, expensive-looking tapestry near the windows opposite the fireplace; a huge, stoneware pot in the corner of one room, below a sagging shelf filled with books that looked to be antiques.

The balcony was so small it was scary, barely large enough to accommodate me, Luca, Daniele, along with Adriana and her quiet, pensive husband who was never introduced, at least not in English. We sat with our knees nearly touching. The balcony cantilevered above the edge of the valley, and the illusion it created was that we sat suspended in the air. Below us, the valley spread out green and lush, despite the wilting heat. In the west, clouds gathered at the head of the valley, pushing a breeze in front of them. Rain was coming. In the light, I saw Adriana better.

She oozed elegance. Her face, wrinkled and spotted with age, was still soft and bright. I could tell that when she was younger, when the Fascists controlled her country, she had been a woman who stole men's gazes. Her former, younger self lurked there, just behind her eyes. Her hands, veined and gnarled a bit with arthritis, moved only when necessary—to punctuate a statement or wave at the hills behind us. When she spoke, her voice rode on an air of intelligence. She constantly cited books and artists, even when she talked about something mundane, like chestnuts.

"She has written a book," Daniele said, interrupting her at one point.

Adriana dismissed his comment with an economic wave of her hand. "It is nothing," she huffed in Italian.

Her husband finally spoke up. *"L'Isola Verde,* that is her book."

I suddenly felt like an imposter, me pretending to be a writer, in the presence of someone who had actually completed a book. I couldn't keep my eyes off Adriana's jewelry. She wore a gold disk around her neck, with a stone set in the middle. The rings on her crooked fingers weren't diamonds, just simple silver bands. On a less elegant woman, this jewelry would seem sparse and out-of-place, but on Adriana, it became somehow perfect, as if the necklace and rings and jangling bracelets had been on her body forever, and the pieces had grown older and more elegant right along with her. I became so transfixed on her jewelry, I forgot to listen to the translations Daniele and Luca argued over. Now and again, I forgot to take notes.

Adriana said she always saw formations of planes flying over Serra during the war, toward Florence or toward the sea. In her memory, it was not unusual to hear engines roaring down the valley. "But the war," she said, "was in Florence and south of us. That's why my mother brought me here. Florence had too much war."

One October day, the sound of one particular engine was different, as the Rhomar circled Serra, smoking and whistling out of control. "It circled Serra like a vulture," she remembered. She had been on this same balcony watching, praying like the villagers for a gust of wind or God's hand to keep the plane away from their mountaintop.

As Adriana talked and remembered, something happened to her eyes. They suddenly fled to another place. She still gazed over the valley, but she was not seeing what we saw. She saw an image that belonged only to her. Men in white parachutes floating over the green valley, dangling like puppets. No, not puppets. Not in her image. For her, they were like the pictures of angels she'd seen in churches. Angels over the valley.

"Quickly, it was quiet," she recalled. "The angels floated in the silence, on the breeze. I watched them until their wings caught in the trees. Angels that fell down to earth. I can still see the angels when I want to," she said.

Adriana brought the villagers' procession to the downed plane into focus with crystallized, specific details: how the women found unused parachutes in the Rhomar and divided up the material for curtains; how men were fascinated by the rubber hoses on the engine. ("Most had never seen hoses before," she said.) Villagers used their donkeys to carry pieces of the plane back to their homes. Over the course of a couple of weeks, the plane decayed to a skeleton of ribs and ash, and soon after that, even the ribs were gone. It struck me as oddly ironic that the plane Adriana compared to a circling vulture had ultimately been picked clean by a band of poor villagers who needed curtains and improvised pot lids.

I began to write like a madman in my notebook, forcing myself to keep my eyes away from Adriana's mesmerizing hands. Daniele and Luca translated in each ear. In an instant, the conversation somehow turned to chestnuts. I hated not being able to pick up segues in Italian. I always felt two steps behind. *So how did you get from the subject of donkeys to chestnuts, Daniele?*

Adriana made shapes in the air with her hands, describing the *metato*, a small room where chestnuts were roasted and cured during the winter months. "We would almost live in the *metato* to keep warm," she said. "The only heat was there." Her husband said they sawed the legs off chairs so they would fit inside the *metato*, under the rising smoke that filtered through the grates filled with chestnuts. "I have good memories of the *metato*," she said. "We smelled like smoke all winter during the war."

Luca repeated a word again and again in my ear. It sounded like a woman's name: Annabelle. I put my palms up in the confusion, the universal sign for about-to-give-up.

"Annabelle?" I said. "Who is she?" More mysterious segues. And what, I wondered to myself, did somebody named Annabelle have to do with chestnuts?

The story was not about a woman, but about a soldier— Hannibal, not Annabelle. *The* Hannibal. The mountains that skirted Serra's valley were the same ones Hannibal crossed with his band of elephants on his way to the Alps. "That," Luca said, "is why there is a zoo on the road to Pistoia. Hannibal left some elephants behind. They have relatives." He smiled and lit a cigarette. The breeze bringing thunderstorms blew the smoke away instantly. I couldn't tell if he was kidding me or not. The others laughed, either at my naiveté or the story of Hannibal's elephant relatives. Maybe both.

I looked over the valley. I saw angels, too. And elephants. And planes like vultures. I was racked with stories. I didn't know which ones to believe, so I chose to believe them all.

NOVANTADUE.

The thunderstorm gutterballed down the valley. The rain followed a path laid down by the lightning and noise, and I heard the wind whistle in the chestnut leaves, the sound like a rasp on a piece of dull metal. It was late, long past midnight.

In my little sleeping loft, I watched through the skylights, watched clouds cover the stars, watched raindrops spackle the glass until sheets of water came too hard to see anything. The storm didn't stop the bells in Serra. Just up the hill, the church rang out the half hour, then ten o'clock, so I knew it had been pouring for a good thirty minutes.

The night of the storm, I was afraid to go to sleep. Usually, I enjoyed the Lortab Technicolor dreams. But lately, something had been stinging me in the night—bedbugs or mosquitoes—leaving tiny constellations of red marks on my legs. And last night, I dreamed about my ex-wife. It was a surprise when I woke up and immediately recalled the dream: We were back in the house she'd abandoned, and she was cleaning manically, rubbing wood until it shone like glass and scouring grout lines on the tile floor. I tried to tell her she didn't live here anymore, but she was having none of it. She told me that she had too much work to do before the house was sold, and I should go check on the children. I told her this wasn't her house now, and she looked at me the way a kindergarten teacher scowls at the kid who misbehaved.

I know where the dream came from. While I was in Serra, my house was on the market back in South Carolina. I was supposed to call the real estate agent every couple of days, but I didn't. I was letting the house take whatever direction it wanted, without my interference. I'd kept the house too long, for all the wrong reasons. It was big and expensive and filled to the joists with memories sharp enough to draw blood. It had taken me two years to put a For Sale sign in the front yard. Now, an ocean away, I just didn't care.

Paolo was renovating his house because a wedding was about to occur. I was selling my house because a marriage evaporated. I couldn't help but grate my teeth at the ironic synchronicity of it all.

I had come here at the perfectly wrong time. Paolo and Renza were in the midst of preparation for Silvia's wedding. The air in their house was thick with anticipation. People broke into giggles for no apparent reason. The wedding hovered over the ex-hotel like a cloud. Life would alter after the wedding. There would be a new body in the house, a lumber man who loved his cigarettes. And he would bring a new smell to the rooms, a new roster of sounds to bounce off the walls. Paolo's house would evolve by simple addition.

Mine had been altered by subtraction. I remembered the day I began taking stock of the things I *wasn't* noticing. It was too quiet in the rooms. The sounds of certain drawers opening was gone. The parade of footsteps in the long hall were minus one set of shoes.

I hoped Paolo and Renza didn't consider me a bad omen for their daughter's wedding. I did feel like I wore the stamp of failure. I'd been limping and sweating in this village for almost two weeks. Most of these people didn't know I was a nice person. The sour woman who swept and cleaned the war memorial each day still wouldn't speak to me in the mornings. I would keep trying. Trying is all we can do at some point. I didn't need to tell that sweeper woman my whole story. I just wanted to say good morning and hear her voice when the reply came.

It was still raining when the Lortab pulled me down and I fell asleep, hoping for no bugs and better dreams.

NOVANTATRÉ.

A driana is not supposed to be here, in this tiny village. She is supposed to be in Florence. In Florence, she would be crossing the stone bridge near her family's house, her hands at her sides, trapping the hem of her shirt against her thighs, so the winds that flow down the Arno in the fall didn't blow it up. She isn't supposed to be here. She is supposed to be walking across the square near the Duomo, watching the men watch her, the soldiers who stare at her the same way they gaze at meatballs and new mail, things they recognize and remember and want.

But Florence has become a confusing city. The Fascists that once walked the city like a new tribe of Medici have doubt in their eyes. She hears more and more rough German in the streets near the gallery, and she grimaces at the coldness of the syllables, the wetness of the monotones. For each person who says Florence will not be shelled, will be spared because of art and history and tradition, there are four more who say it is a fool who trusts any man with a bomb beneath his thumb.

Confusion and danger, danger and doubt. Adriana's mother insisted they leave. She took Adriana away from Florence into the mountains to the west, away from the museums and the paper shops, away from the bread stores and the churches. Now, Adriana stands on the balcony of the family's summer home in Serra, a house at the end of the tiny lane that leads from the square, past the church. Her mother has brought her to a town that bores twenty-year olds like Adriana. There are no men whistling at her here, no boys on *bicycles offering her rides across the river. Only mountains and a big, burning bird in the sky above her.*

Adriana thinks the plane looks like a vulture, a vulture with its tail feathers on fire. The plane circles the mountains as if it is searching for something. From her spot high on the balcony, Adriana can see people below, near the village square, scurrying for their houses, grabbing children from the stone road and pulling them close. Everyone watches the plane and tries to steer it away from the village with their eyes before they close their doors on the sky. That is why no one notices the angels.

But Adriana does. Floating down to the earth, through the smoke and clouds, are nine angels, nine white-winged angels drifting in the breeze that swirls above the valley.

Decades later, the angels are what Adriana will remember most. "They made things quiet," she will say. "I know the noise was still there, but these things, these white things in the sky, they took the sounds away."

Nine men jump from the plane when the last of the B-17's engines flame out. Nine white parachutes against the green-gray of the mountain slopes. "I knew what they were," Adriana will recall. "Men dangling in the air, but I thought they looked like angels. They floated like angels should float."

Adriana watches the angels sift into the valley. Her mother calls her from inside the house, but Adriana doesn't answer. She keeps counting parachutes with her finger. Still nine. Behind her, on the western side of the mountain, the vulture circles still, Guilfoil tucked in its belly.

Suddenly, over the mountains from the east, a small, quick plane appears. The cross on its side means it belongs to the Germans. The airplane seems to dart, then banks and rolls, bearing down on the angels. The dangling men can't will themselves to fall faster. They kick their legs and try to make themselves heavier. Adriana hears noise again, the scream of a smaller airplane, the pop of a gun firing at the angels, over and over. The small plane circles, levels out and fires more, then repeats. The angels pull their legs up, to make themselves smaller. One angel doesn't move at all. And the small plane disappears in the direction it came. The vulture

*careens into the western slope. And Adriana watches angels
light in the trees. Some of them dangle there in plain sight,
some disappear into the thick canopy of the forest.*

*The angels. She will see them always, whenever she closes
her eyes and thinks about the valley and the war and the time
the war took her away from Florence.*

NOVANTAQUATTRO.

Each time Daniele and Luca told me they had another interview scheduled and glanced uphill from the village square, my knee began to ache. An interview up the hill meant a walk back down, a walk which would bring gravity and body weight to bear on my bone-bare joint.

Walking was a daily comedy. By now, my limp was so pronounced, I bobbed like a shorebird when I moved from point A to B. (In fact, during my little vacation to the coast, I went for a short walk to my car to grab a book, and the hotel security guard stopped me at the door. He said in broken, elementary English that I shouldn't go into the street drunk, that the police were likely to pick me up. I was stone-cold sober, but my knee had given me a gait like a morning wino.)

This afternoon, they said there was a woman up the hill I definitely needed to see before I left. Yet another Parenti. Parenti was one of the founding families of Serra. I learned this from a framed reproduction of an etching on Paolo's wall, just below a taxidermied deer. My ex-wife's family was in the Parenti line. No matter how I tried to avoid it, I noticed how many people in the village had her nose. Or vice versa. Paolo, for sure, had it. And several of the women who gathered around the card table. Even the sweeper-woman who glared at me from the war memorial suggested my ex-wife when she turned slightly in profile. It was like being haunted daily by the ghost of someone who wasn't dead yet.

The house was almost to the top of the hill, just beyond the church and only a few doors down from Adriana's. Michelina

Parenti greeted us at the door, and I immediately recognized her. I'd seen her in a half dozen places in the village. She flitted around her house, pinballing from room to room to bring us wine and photo albums. With her bright, white hair, she was like a flash of lightning zooming in and out of rooms. When she sat, she still moved, bouncing her knees or moving her head side-to-side, bird-like.

Michelina didn't have much personal knowledge of Guilfoil and the plane crash. But she knew a great deal about Serra during the war years. After she poured us glasses of cold wine, she leafed through photo albums packed with grainy, sepia photos from decades ago. In the pictures, I saw Paolo's house from the days when it was a hotel and the convent that ultimately became my apartment building. Michelina repeated many of the stories I'd already heard as we crowded into her small living room. Claudio had come with Daniele and Luca. Claudio pulled out a cigarette, and Michelina fired some harsh Italian at him, chasing the pack of smokes back into his pocket. He blushed like an accused schoolboy.

I found myself getting very comfortable, what with Michelina's wine and the softness of her couch. Her voice—in whatever language she chose; she spoke several—featured a constant lilt, up and down the possibilities of inflection. I lapsed into borderline hypnosis, listening to her stories about Serra during the Occupation, when Fascists and Nazis roamed the mountain roads between Montecatini Terme and Abetone (a ski village farther up the mountain) searching for deserters and enemies and young men hiding from war.

I took notes, but I listened more, gliding up and down with Michelina's voice. Claudio and Luca kept their glasses full. Michelina offered me several old postcards that pictured Serra sometime before the war. The one single automobile in the foreground of one of the cards looked like a model from the '30s. I tried to refuse the cards, but she insisted. I took a breath, a deep one, letting the wine and the Lortab (did I mention I'd popped a couple before the walk up the hill?) and the stories wash over me.

Michelina put her hand on my leg. "I am sorry," she said. I thought she meant it was time for us to go, so I shifted on the couch and closed my notebook. I may have glanced at my watch, as if I had somewhere to be. Daniele didn't take the hint.

"We should go," I said.

"No, no, no," Michelina sang out. "I am sorry for all the work you are doing."

I was confused. Michelina was speaking English, but I looked to Daniele for help, which made no sense. He shrugged and sipped.

"*Non capisco*," I said to her. I didn't understand.

"Ah," she said, "and you are exactly right. You do not understand. You can never understand what it was like when the Fascists were here. You can never understand the soldiers in my street. You have no memory of the Occupation."

I wanted to tell her that in lieu of memory, I was talking to people like her, but Michelina didn't give me a chance to answer. She fluttered around the room as she talked.

"You cannot tell this story," she said, and I felt a chill begin in my scalp. Even though she was moving, her eyes never left mine. "You cannot tell it because you can never understand. I think you have wasted your time. You cannot tell this. You will fail."

She was near enough to pat me on the shoulder in the manner you'd pacify a scared animal. "I am sorry for you," she said, and she smiled so warmly, you would have thought we were related.

We left then, and on the way down the hill to my apartment, I'm sure my knee ached and I limped like an afflicted man, but I didn't remember anything other than the throbbing, heavy feeling Michelina had just planted in my chest.

NOVANTACINQUE.

Another sleepless night. Michelina's words ran like an audio loop in my head. *You cannot tell this story. You cannot tell this story.* I remembered Dr. Morton and his haze of cigarette smoke and his advice that I should go to law school, that I could never write because I hadn't suffered. He was probably laughing now, somewhere. I stared at the stars through the skylight. I wanted to march back up the hill and tell Michelina that I was suffering for this goddamn story. Every step I took hurt. Every time I looked around the square in Serra and saw the bridge of my ex-wife's nose on her distant, distant relatives, my heart clutched like a machine about to come to a grinding halt.

And I had Guilfoil. *Was* Guilfoil. I understood him and he understood me. I could appropriate his feeling of sudden mortality. I don't know why I felt the need to convince some twitching, white-haired woman that I wasn't wasting my time and somebody else's money.

I hopped one-legged down the spiral stairs to the bathroom and checked my Lortab stash. I could spare another tonight to help me sleep. I wanted the Lortab dreams, big-budget Technicolor dreams that lasted well into morning. I wanted something else in my head right now. I wanted to forget for a while the things I couldn't hope to accomplish.

NOVANTASEI.

Daniele and Luca felt sorry for me. They didn't understand the value of being alone. To them, solitude was a disease. They were stunned I planned to spend my final Saturday night in my apartment reading and writing. They invited me to have dinner with them, down the mountain at a restaurant called Zacco. And they insisted that I drive. Probably to give me a sense of worth. Or perhaps just get them there and back.

Zacco was several notches higher on the atmosphere meter than Il Poggiolino. White cloths draped the tables and the wood trim on the walls and ceiling shone like it was wet. I originally thought Daniele and Luca had, on the spur of a merciful moment, asked me to dinner by themselves. I soon discovered I was an add-on to an existing plan, which was completely fine by me. By this time, I had grown accustomed to being the stranger.

I followed Daniele through the restaurant to a long, loud table situated conveniently beneath a small television set mounted on the wall. The ubiquitous World Cup was on. Two teams, neither of them Italy, ran back and forth across the corner of the room.

It was a large group. I sat next to Marco, an ad executive from Florence who spoke passable English and almost choked on his wine when he found out I'd been in the advertising business for years and years. He immediately asked why we had no naked women in our ads in America. At least that's what I thought he said. Lorenzo, a loud, smiley man across the table was married to a French woman he'd left at home "to be pregnant," Luca said. Luca was more enthusiastic about Lorenzo's missing French wife than about Lorenzo himself, so I assumed she was gorgeous. Mario and Laura were a married couple to my right. It turned out Mario was the distant nephew of Antonluigi, the man who first gave me Guilfoil's story. Mario had never heard of Guilfoil or the Rhomar. He couldn't keep his eyes off the television, constantly letting his gaze rise to the action on the screen. Claudio was there, too, excusing himself every few minutes to step outside and smoke a cigarette. (It turned out that Italy had not banned smoking in restaurants. Rather, the government required eating establishments to install a mega-expensive, ultra-complicated ventilation/filtration system, if they wanted to allow customers to smoke inside. Very few restaurant owners could actually afford the ventilators, so in essence, smoking was ingeniously outlawed.)

And Simone, the large lumberjack, sat directly at the head of the table and had control of the waiter, whom everyone at the table seemed to know. Daniele and Luca sat far enough away, I couldn't depend on them for translations. Marco was some help, but for the most part, I had to fend for myself.

I realized my Italian was getting better. Being immersed in Serra for close to three weeks had finally given me the ability to follow some of the conversations. I mean, I understood that Lorenzo's wife was moody and mad at him most of the time. That Mario had a good bit of money riding on the soccer match, which explained his obsession with the television. That Marco couldn't understand the American fear of breasts and loins. Bits and pieces of conversation came at me like shrapnel. Once, when I got up to use the bathroom, Marco saw me limping, and when I sat back down, he asked in English if I was hurt. I was able to reply in Italian that I had an arthritic knee. He seemed impressed at my attempt to talk to him in his own language.

But I didn't confess to him that the knee conversation was one of the dialogues I'd rehearsed in my apartment. I'd begun to do that on a regular basis. I would sit at my little kitchen table with my dictionary and imagine scenarios in which I might be an actor. I practiced what I might say to the old woman sweeping the leaves from the war memorial. Or I'd stand shaving, rehearsing how I would ask Paolo if I could work with him in his garden one day or if we could have some fried zucchini flowers for dinner. And of course, I created simple Italian monologues about my ex-wife and her Pierced Partner.

Practicing certain scenarios also meant that I steered the conversations in the direction of my rehearsals. If I asked Sonia at the *negozio* about focaccia and she replied about the thunder the night before, I was screwed. It struck me that rehearsing the conversations I might have was the worst kind of storytelling. Instead of letting the world unfurl in front of me, I was trying to corral it into a scene for which I already knew the ending. Sure, it was all the result of fear— fear of looking stupid, but maybe in one way, it was truly smart, almost genius-like.

That night at Zacco, I'd prepared only a half dozen little dialogues: where I was from, what I was doing here, why I limped, something about my children, why I wasn't married and as a brave icebreaker, something about how well Italy had done in the World Cup. I wasn't prepared for Marco's Italo-English dissertation on breasts or Lorenzo's marriage difficulties or Mario's fear of his bookie. So I listened as best I could and acted somewhat like a child, speaking only when spoken to.

NOVANTASETTE.

I was saved by food. Simone, who fashioned himself an amateur gastronome, ordered the antipasti for us. Plates of mild, white cheeses and slices of pear, all of it drizzled with brown chestnut honey. In shallow ramekins, pieces of melted, baked brie lay atop heavily-oiled bread, which was then draped with thin slices of a strong ham I couldn't identify. In a matching dish, the oil-soaked bread was covered with warm goat cheese, all hidden beneath ribbons of prosciutto. Bowls of olives soaking in their oil. Crostini misto with toast made from bread that tasted like it had risen and browned only minutes before. And too-hot-to-touch bowls of cooked farrow laced with tomatoes and onions.

These appetizers took almost an hour to pass and share. The wine seemed to be in lockstep with the food—cold Pinot Grigio with the meats and cheeses and a heavier red table wine with the olives and misto.

The waiter cleared the carnage from the antipasti and brought the primi. I couldn't remember what I had ordered; the wine had dulled my head. He slid a plate in front of me and said, "*Tortelli de potate*," and that sounded somewhat familiar. The tortellini and potatoes melted away in my mouth like cotton candy. The rest of the table spooned a sample of their pasta on my plate. I had ravioli and penne, farfalle and fusilli. My stomach began to give way.

More wine. Bottles of Chianti that felt slightly colder than room temperature and a table wine from the vineyard just on the other side of the mountain from Serra. I looked for the rooster on the Chianti label and found him. A rooster meant it was the real deal, real Chianti from Chianti. Secundi came on the heels of the wine replenishment. I ate wild boar, but I sampled everyone's—the bloody-rare steak, the fish, the roasted rabbit.

I'd never eaten food like this, plate after plate that I could never create in my own kitchen. I knew I could try, but would never replicate the taste of that particular slice of cheese on that particular pear with that kind of honey again. It would never be the same.

There was a scattering of desserts—tiramisu and ice cream and a plate of fruit and cheeses—but no one's heart was in it. We were all too full and too tired to chew. But Simone, however, decided we were not beyond simple swallowing, so he ordered bottles of limoncello and Muscat and grappa. The topography of the table changed and suddenly the white linen was dotted with small café glasses full of the aperitifs. "For our digestion!" Luca yelled as he threw back a shot of grappa.

The limoncello was straight from the freezer and left a cold trail down my throat, while the Muscat lingered sweet in my mouth. We took the bottles outside, with the owner's permission, and sat on the small stone wall in front of Zacco's, watching the road and the sky.

This meal, this four-hour marathon of taste and smell and touch was, I knew, not a story in itself. It was only a scene. It had no narrative, no climax. But I knew it was an important part of my story in Serra. I had just hung out with friends—brand new friends, sure, but friends nonetheless—and eaten until I could barely move. I had talked with them in Italian. I had been unafraid to use hand signals to get my words across. I felt like I belonged at the table, finally.

NOVANTOTTO.

The day of the Italy-Germany World Cup match. I heard people talking about it in the village. The conversations were more animated than usual, more hand-wringing and more roller coasters of inflection. That morning, I watched a couple of boys kicking a soccer ball against the high wall at the war memorial. Together, they vanquished an imaginary Germania, cheering themselves much to the scowling disgust of the sour woman who swept the plateau of the statue above them.

All three of them caught me staring from my bench in the sun. I waved and followed with a loud *"Buongiorno!"* The boys waved back and the woman snarled. It was going to be hot. Thick, humid air, too thick for these mountains, had settled into the valley during the night and refused to burn off as the morning ticked by. I quietly wished for the sour woman to fall off the memorial and lay there, baking on the stones. I was in a bad mood. I hadn't had my breakfast Lortab yet and my knee was screaming, even when I sat still. They were expecting me at Il Poggiolino that night. I had the whole day to get myself ready.

NOVANTANOVE.

I opened the windows of the apartment to confuse the swallows as they dove into the final hatch of insects for the day. I took a shower and shaved, then spent a couple of minutes deciding which pants to wear, and I realized I was getting ready for a date.

I hated myself for that. The people at Il Poggiolino were simply being nice. For all I knew, they felt sorry for me, and here I was, putting a new label on the event. All because of the Glistening Pizza Cook. I imagined sitting next to her, the two of us watching the screen, her skin cooling off, after hours in the gape of the pizza oven. In fact, by this time, I had convinced myself that the pizza cook had secretly requested my presence at the restaurant. I had become a master of delusion, which I supposed was a result of too much solitude and Lortab and lingering bachelorhood.

But the fact is, I hated the idea of dating. Until my divorce, I had thought of dating as this phase that had served its purpose and gone away, like a fad. Dating was bellbottoms or Beta tape—important and useful at the time, but ultimately forgettable. Once she left, however, I was dragged kicking and screaming back into a pair of metaphorical, ill-fitting bellbottoms. I had been set up with women who were scouring the landscape for husbands, with women who hated men and had their sights trained on revenge, with women who wanted someone to listen to their stories. (I didn't mind listening to stories. But usually if I appeared interested, I was dubbed sensitive and compassionate and a candidate for category number one, see above.) For a while,

Scott Gould

I dated to get laid. Then things flip-flopped and I got laid in order to date. That was when I went a little nuts and locked myself in my house for a few weeks. And the whole time, I blamed her, the One Who Left. When she moved out, she already had a steady boyfriend. She built up a big head start without me knowing it. And I wasn't good, running from behind.

CENTO.

I was not the only person invited to Il Poggiolino for the match. An older couple who seemed like family sat in the corner. A table of young men, all of them wearing heavy five o'clock shadows, sat at one side of a long table, each of them facing the television like a panel of judges. The owner saw me walk in and said much too loud that Germany had arrived. I smiled while the room laughed. The hair I still possessed had turned blonder because of my trip to the coast. I did look a bit German, I had to admit. The fire still wavered in the brick oven, the pizza cook glowing and standing watch over the coals. She didn't turn around to look at *the German.* The owner locked the door behind me, while I gave the crowd a wave and tried hard not to make it look like a Nazi salute.

Before I left the apartment, I had swallowed a Lortab with a large Peroni chaser, and the combo package hit when I entered the restaurant. The scene took on a shimmering quality, as if viewed through antique glass. Everyone smiled at me because I must have been unavoidably loveable. Loveable and immortal and brave. I thought about leaping the bar and grabbing the pizza cook by her slick upper arms and kissing her dark hairline, low on her neck. Instead, I sat down at a table by myself, behind the panel of judges.

The waitress, who was off-duty and frankly a little perturbed that I might be a customer needing attention, told me in Italglish that food service was over, but the bar would be open during the match. *Oh, good,* I thought. *More beer is perfect. Just what I need.* So I ordered a media DAP and settled in, keeping the pizza cook locked in my peripheral vision. She looked as though she'd been in the sun. I imagined her on a beach. Or in her garden, her apron tucked full of zucchini and tomatoes.

Italy was winning. I had missed their first goal, but the second brought on a roar that surprised me. I didn't think a group this small could create that kind of noise. The old couple were about to have sympathetic strokes. They jumped and grabbed each other between screams. I think the panel was cursing in Italian, but happy cursing. The pizza cook turned and smiled at the screen. Her teeth were perfect.

The match continued and the pizza cook kept ducking in a back room, then reappearing at the bar for a moment before retreating to the heat and the coals. I didn't see anything cooking, so I couldn't imagine why she needed to tend her fire. Maybe it was just habit. I tried to time my bathroom trips with her ins-and-outs, so I could perhaps catch her at the bar. I had to be careful. I wasn't sure whether or not she was the owner's daughter. I didn't want to piss off any fathers. The room grew cloudy, not from the beer and Lortab, but because the no-smoking rule was obviously for business hours only. On my last trip down the stairs to the bathroom, I noticed I had on the Italian sandals-that-broke-the-marriage's-back. That seemed suitable. They even felt as though they fit better this evening.

I climbed back up the stairs slowly, mentally timing my arrival in the dining room. I had practiced several scenarios with my Italian phrasebook that afternoon, lines from the "Ah, Amore!" section. I felt confident I could introduce myself to the pizza cook, tell her how beautiful she was, ask her if she would like to come up the mountain with me.

I took a last clean breath before I entered the smoke bank. Suddenly, the pizza cook stood a yard in front of me, her hair down now, falling between her shoulder blades. But she didn't pause. She headed straight for the front door. So she could unlock it. For her husband and children.

On one of her trips to the kitchen, she'd put her wedding ring back on her finger. I supposed it was too silly and dangerous to slide pizzas in and out of the fire with a piece of metal around your finger. Two little girls, dark-haired and quiet, wrapped themselves around their mom's legs. The husband ignored her and made a bee-line to the beer taps. He called out to no one in particular about the score, and one of the experts said, "*Due nil,*" and the husband squeezed by the rest of his family on the way to the television, placing a hand on his wife's rear end to steady himself.

I was the one who needed steadying. I was suddenly thirteen again, at the Youth Center dance, watching the girl I hoped to dance with walk out the door with an eighth grader. I had rehearsed the dialogue, created scenes. I had sketched the story board in my head, but the reality of her life was a husband with a forty-inch waist and two little daughters with eyes dark as ink spots.

I sat as inconspicuously as possible, rummaged in my pocket for my emergency Lortab. My knees didn't really hurt. The pain had moved north and deeper, away from the bone and into the gut. I drank my last DAP as the match ended. Italy would play in the World Cup finals. I thanked the owner for his invitation and promised to come again soon for pizza. On the dark, thin road up the mountain, I heard car horns blowing and screaming soccer fans celebrating. I couldn't see them. They were deep in the hills somewhere. In fact, the night was strangely black. There must have been a new moon.

CENTOUNO.

On the road between Il Poggiolino and Serra, from the shoulder of the road, a man ran out of the darkness into the beams of my headlights. He was naked, except for the Italian flag streaming from his neck like a superhero's cape. His ass shone white in the light. He sprinted across the asphalt and dove into the darkness on the opposite side of the road.

On any other night, I would have laughed.

CENTODUE.

There was no road kill in Italy, at least none I could spot. I drove the switchbacks between Montecatini and Serra a dozen times and the long slope between Pistoia and Serra a couple of round trips, and I even walked the road from Serra past the cemetery to the first intersection pointing toward Panacagliora, and I never, *never* saw the first sign of road sacrifice. I'm from the South, where road kill is a tourist attraction. We I.D. the dead, even when they have become the size of a manila folder. But here? Here, road kill seemed to be an endangered species.

Maybe, I thought, road crews patrolled the pavement in the early morning light and scraped the roads clean. Where I come from, that task was normally left to buzzards and possums and the more famished stray dogs. I did have a friend who once bragged of having installed a compartment onto the firewall of his truck where he heated road kill on long trips. He said one time, he slow-roasted a woodchuck on a haul from Spartanburg, S.C. to South Florida.

Once I noticed the lack of road kill, I began to watch the road more carefully. I found a shady turn-out where I could park and observe what the road might bring me. Every Tuesday and Thursdays, a cycling club climbed by in the early morning. All of the riders were men—older men, the youngest probably around sixty-five or so. No one wore a helmet. They tapped out a cadence that defied their ages, hammering against gravity and the years as they leaned against the slope.

I'd already wondered what it would be like to cycle this

mountain, and I quickly put the thought to rest. I'd bonk a couple dozen kilometers out of Montecatini. I wasn't a good climber, and at just over two hundred pounds, I was large for a run up this hill. But these guys had twenty, twenty-five years on me. Their arms were skinny and muscle-less, their shoulders rounded and worn down. But their legs, their damn legs were pistons—shaved and vein-popping. They waved when they rode by, probably saying to themselves, *Look, an American sitting on his ass. What else is new?*

I perched there on the hood of my rental car, imagining myself at sixty-five. I always assumed I'd be married, hanging out with grandchildren, teasing my wife about her new haircut—the wife I'd had for close to forty years. She and I wouldn't have to talk much because we knew each other so well. We would have developed our own language of hand signals and eyebrow lifts. And that picture, I realized all along, was as clichéd as a knock-knock joke. It was the image most men have of their last years: total comfort and contentment.

However, there on the mountainside, I watched men glide up the grade, and I looked down at my bare feet crossed under me. The divorce sandals lay on the ground by the tire. In that moment, I felt no better than road kill, run over by my own peek into the future. I had not allowed for change, hadn't checked the wind enough. I had assumed too much, maybe, and the twist in the story left me flattened on the asphalt.

I hated metaphors, but here one was, riding by me on the way to the summit: men who just kept climbing and climbing, without protection, without any hint of fear. They would never become road kill.

CENTOTRÉ.

Serra was a village of sameness. The buses arrived at the
War Memorial at the same time each day. The church
bells never varied, ringing out the full and half hours. Each
morning at nine o'clock, Sonia rolled up the metal security door at the *negozio*. Nothing went off the rails, nobody
stepped across the line. And when there was an unusual
sound in the village, chances were it was bad news.

One afternoon I listened to the thin wail of an ambulance
float out of the valley below my apartment. The siren grew
louder and more desperate as it roared into Serra, the ambulance going as fast as possible down the main street, then
up the narrow, stone road past the church. I found out later
a woman, a very old woman who would have been young
and alive the day Guilfoil came to earth, had been stung
by bees and died of an allergic reaction. The irony made
me shake my head. To live nearly a century and tend your
flower baskets until a bee, one that was probably looking
for chestnut blossoms but got waylaid by the color of the
woman's dress, planted its stinger in a fold of old skin.

Daniele said when he was a boy, some twenty years ago,
he came to Serra every weekend during the summers. He
stayed weeks at a time with his aunts and uncles. He and
his friends played soccer on a pitch just above the village,
one of the only flat pieces of land, near the olive groves.
He said they would stay out all day and would have to be
dragged back to the village, even after the sun had dropped
behind the mountains.

"Now," he said, "there is no football. The pitch is a landing
place for a helicopter, in case there is a medical emergency."

Scott Gould

"Like the woman and the bee?" I asked.

"She," he said, smiling, "was probably just ready to die. I don't think she wanted to ride in a helicopter."

Or maybe, she thought young boys still played football on the grass near the olives.

CENTOQUATTRO.

Fourth of July, and I was probably the only person in Serra who cared. Before I went to Sonia's to buy some bread and salami for lunch, I practiced a dialogue in which I'd tell her that today was a big holiday back in the States. I looked up the Italian words for *fireworks* and *independence*.

When I heard her roll open the metal doors, I gave her a couple of minutes to settle in, then walked the fifty yards to her store. In the middle of explaining Independence Day, the crotchety lady, the War Memorial Cleaner, walked in and a cloud filled the *negozio*, her sour attitude fouling the sunlight streaming through the open door. I smiled even bigger and told her the same story. Big Day. Lots of fireworks. Bad British. (They liked that part. Sonia smiled when I said something disparaging about the Brits.) The other woman ignored me and flipped through an Italian gossip magazine.

What I didn't tell the ladies was, I remembered another July 4th:

Three years earlier—three years to the day—my wife and I flew back to the States from a trip to Italy, to Serra. I recalled her acting especially happy on the flight back, chatting up the attendants and ordering more cocktails than usual. I, on the other hand, felt as though the minute we broke through the clouds and began to descend, I would see some sort of omen about the impending events, buildings with funnels of smoke rising from their ashes or a mountain of mud sliding into a river. This was the end of the trip. *When we get back from Italy, I'm leaving you.* That's what she'd said a few weeks before. The clock had run out. And there was no anti-aircraft flak popping outside the window. I wouldn't spiral down like Guilfoil. I wouldn't be pulled, smoking, from the belly of this airplane.

Three years ago, we'd landed in Atlanta, and while we waited in line to clear customs, my soon-to-be-estranged wife went off to the bathroom. She said she would call our girls and let them know we were close to home. I found out months later that one of the first things she did was call The Pierced Guy. The Pepper Shaker. She made her phone call on Independence Day.

Now, it seemed like a bad movie scene. I wondered if she even alluded to the date when she heard his voice on the phone. "Happy Independence Day!" she probably said, fireworks in her voice, while I stood in line, hoping silently that I would never get back into the country. She made a phone call. *Happy Independence Day.*

I didn't attempt to explain this to Sonia and the sour woman. But I did wish them a good day, perhaps more enthusiastically than was required. I walked back into the sun and the morning heat rising from the street. I decided I would spend the rest of my Independence Day writing about Guilfoil and watching swallows play in the breeze, and I would force myself to be happy. And if that didn't work, I still had a handful of Lortabs and a large bottle of Peroni in the refrigerator.

CENTOCINQUE.

I needed to see Lorenza one last time. I had an excuse: I wanted to transfer some of my Euros back into dollars before I left. And for some silly reason, I wanted to tell Lorenza goodbye. She'd occupied so many minutes of my thinking-time in Serra. I felt I owed her something. Closure, perhaps. (There was that word again.) Now, after days and days in the village full of my ex-wife's relatives, I was no closer to understanding closure that I'd been before I came to Italy. In fact, I wasn't sure if closure was a bad or good thing. But I had that young romantic's ache in my chest, like I was back at that same middle-school dance and I had to tell (needed to tell, was *dying* to tell) that eighth-grade girl that I really, really liked her, before the adults snapped on the lights and put away the Sprite punch.

The heat was so brutal, I'd begun to sweat during the walk from my car to the bank's revolving door. Lorenza's scooter was nowhere in sight, but I was sure she was behind the counter. I'd seen her head flashing blonde through the glass. I pressed the button outside, and Lorenza hesitated a moment before she reached down and buzzed me in. In all likelihood, she waited because I was an unfamiliar face and, by extension, somewhat suspicious. But I like to imagine her hesitancy was caused by her breath catching the moment she laid eyes on me. *Scrittore is back!*

The Pink Panther shirt was not on display that afternoon. In its place, Lorenza wore a wildly patterned t-shirt—maybe the Italian equivalent of tie-dye—that clung to her like a coat of paint, tucking ultimately into a pair of jeans that rode low on her hips. I could see all of this when she moved from the counter to her teller stand, a short few steps that seemed, from my point of view, a chance for Lorenza to display herself. I couldn't tell if she was flirting with me or simply walking from here to there, and the fact that I couldn't distinguish one from the other almost brought tears to my eyes. I was getting old, with an overactive imagination. And that was a sad way for a man to be.

Silvia was not at my side, so I was flying solo as far as the Italian language was concerned. But surely I would be able to communicate with Lorenza without words. Just by staring at me, she could tell how sorry I was I'd followed her home that afternoon or how enamored I was with her ability to wear a shirt three sizes too small or how lonely I was after all that time in the village, lonely for someone—okay, not just someone, but a woman, specifically, the one in front of me.

I stared at her, trying my best to talk to her with my eyes until I realized I still had on my sunglasses. She might have thought I was blind. When I removed them, the room grew instantly brighter and Lorenza stood, waiting for my request. "*Dollari?*" I asked, holding out a stack of Euros. Lorenza laughed at me.

Before her laugh faded, I had an epiphany: traveling alone, in a country where you don't speak the language, brings the worst of you to the surface. All of your weaknesses, every foible that you can somehow bury by blathering and posing and tap dancing in your native tongue, rises like something bloated and drowned. When you cannot talk, when you cannot protest or debate, you see yourself in a brighter, clearer light. Now, I saw how badly I communicated with women, standing there in front of Lorenza with my little offering wavering between us. I realized how much of a puppy dog I was, panting after something I wanted instead of making a plan, instead of taking real steps forward. It was instantly clear that I was one of those people in the world that let things happen, rather than make them happen.

I was Guilfoil. I hadn't been shot in the head, but I was riding a plane into the trees, hoping the engines would refire and get me back to altitude. And, as I stood there, staring at Lorenza's face but not seeing it, I realized that in the years since my wife left, I had always been like Guilfoil, hoping someone would take what remained after the crash and make something useful with the leftovers.

To her credit, Lorenza could see I was having trouble. She didn't press forward, didn't attempt to hurry me. "I need some dollars," I said in English, abandoning the Italian. "I'm going home tomorrow. Back to the United States. I have to go back to work soon. I'm a teacher. I mean, I teach some. I write too." I rambled, filling all the potential silences.

"*Si, si*," she said. "*Va bene*." She hadn't understood a word, except maybe my need for some money. I had nothing more to say. She wouldn't understand a word of any confession I tendered about following her home that afternoon. I stood there, naked without a language. It all came down to money. Simple business. I handed her my Euros and she handed back bills with familiar faces. They were the first Americans I'd seen in weeks. I felt a little homesick.

I knew I had to end this part of the story, had to end the Lorenza chapter, even if she didn't realize it. There was no way I could have driven down the mountain without ever stepping inside the bank. Lorenza asked me something, probably if I needed anything else.

Italian suddenly popped into my head. "*Dove è tuo motorino?*" Where was her scooter? She cocked her head again.

"Eh?" she said, and I repeated my question and smiled. Her eyes hardened. She was speaking with them, now. They were asking, *Why the hell do you want to know about my scooter?* She glanced around me, toward the street. *What have you done with my scooter?* the eyes said.

"No, no, I haven't done anything with your motorino. Seriously. I was just asking," I said, now in English. "Just making conversation." I tried smiling again, but it fell flat on my lips, I'm sure. Lorenza rattled off some Italian. She looked at my hands for some reason, as if they contained evidence. The stack of tens and twenties lay in my palm. Then, she called a name out. It sounded like Pilar or Pillo, and a large man in a suit the size of a pup tent, appeared from an office behind the counter. Lorenza rattled off more sentences, nodding at me while she talked. I heard the word *Americano* and *motorino*, and when it filtered through my paranoia-translator, I knew I had possibly become the American who stole Lorenza's scooter. I held up my hand to protest and the bills rained to the floor, fluttering in a half dozen directions like birds landing. When I ducked to gather them, I lost sight of Lorenza and Pillar-man for a moment, but when I rose—my money tight in my fist again—they were still there, behind the counter, balanced on their toes slightly to see where I'd gone.

I couldn't protest. I didn't have the words, except "Goodbye, Lorenza." I spun on my heels and took off toward the revolving door. I didn't look back, just headed for the exit, which was bathed in stinging bright sunlight, glare so stunning, I couldn't find the handle. I just pushed hard on something that felt like glass and hoped it wouldn't break. It gave way and rotated toward the light, and I limped into the glare without looking back.

Only when I got to my car and sank into the seat did I realize I'd left my sunglasses on the counter in front of Lorenza. I wondered if they made their way to a lost-and-found box or to Lorenza's house. Either way, I was glad I left them with her. It wasn't really closure. It was something better.

CENTOSEI.

I wanted to be through with Guilfoil. I'd found out as much as I could about how he went down and the trouble he'd caused in the forest. I'd heard about angels over the valley and men dangling from chestnut trees like puppets. I'd had a woman tell me to give up chasing Guilfoil, that I didn't have the ability to tell a story I'd never seen with my own eyes. I had what I needed for the Surdna people. A couple of notebooks crammed with notes and quotations. I could give them an essay, no worries. I could even make some things up.

I was leaving tomorrow, on an early afternoon flight out of Florence. My last dinner in Italy wasn't a celebration at Il Poggiolino or Zacco's. Paolo and Renza invited me to their house for supper. I knew Renza would do nothing special, and that was fine by me. When you ate dinner at Paolo and Renza's, the only thing she altered was the number of plates at the table.

I walked from the old convent to Paolo's ex-hotel carrying a large gift bag. I'd bought Silvia and Stefano a wedding gift, a nice frame they could hang in their newly renovated apartment.

The grouchy War Memorial Sweeper sat on the bench outside the pastry shop. She studied her feet as if they were about to do a trick. I cleared my throat and said, in my best Italian, *"Buona sera."* She looked at me and cocked her head as if I'd insulted one of her relatives. And she didn't answer. I'd done so well gathering the Guilfoil information, but I'd been an utter failure in so many areas. Lorenza was a stranger. And the Memorial Woman treated me like a leper.

Inside Paolo's house, Renza scurried between the kitchen and dining room, dealing out plates and tiny café glasses that Paolo filled with wine he'd retrieved from the basement. Stefano sat in one corner, admiring his smoke rings. I knew if I came back in a decade, he'd still be there, puffing. He'd established his place in the house. It would never change. Until, that is, somebody died. That always caused a reshuffling.

Vivetta was feeling better. She settled her tiny little body on the sofa, below a line of taxidermied, anxious deer. I gave her a hug as softly as I knew how, but I still felt the bird-like bones in her shoulders shift under my hands. Her voice was as thin and reedy as her body when she asked me how I was doing.

We gathered around the table. Silvia wanted to know how the research was going, how Daniele and Luca had worked out. Renza passed the *risotto con funghi* and the sautéed mushroom caps, porcinis Paolo had gathered on a hillside "not far from the *selva dell'apparecchio*," Silvia said. Stefano crushed his cigarette out and said something about Italy and the World Cup, and everyone at the table nodded with a solemnity usually reserved for talk about deceased relatives. The eggplant parmigiana made its way around the table. Italy was the only place in the world I could stomach eggplant. When I tried it in the States, it always seemed to be missing an ingredient.

Between bites—using his daughter as a translator—Paolo told me I should talk to his friend, Giampiero, before I left town. Paolo said Giampiero had a piece of the plane in his house, and he used it as a fireplace iron for cooking. I knew of Giampiero. I'd met him briefly on my previous trips to Serra. If Paolo was the unofficial mayor of Serra, Giampiero was its chamber of commerce. He had a bright, toothy smile constantly plastered on his face, and he told me animated stories that he found insanely funny, but I couldn't understand. Giampiero's Italian was so fast and hammered together, he sounded like he was humming instead of talking.

Paolo wanted me to talk to Giampiero right then, during

dinner. Renza shot Paolo a look that could draw blood, so Paolo only went to the door and hollered into the darkness for Giampiero. An answer floated back, out of the black. I guessed they communicated like that a lot. A few more calls into the shadows on the street, and I had an appointment early the next morning, before I left for Florence.

CENTOSETTE.

I was nervous the entire dinner. This was my last chance to explain to Paolo and his family exactly what had happened with the *freddo* ex-wife. My last chance to lob a grenade or two onto her reputation. My little Italian revenge. The trip was coming to a close, so earlier that day, I had practiced my little speech. I had tried to figure out a way to explain to them what a pierced penis was. (A way to tell them without using pantomime.) I wanted to take at least one more decent stab at making myself feel better. I didn't know that Paolo and Renza and Silvia had been rehearsing something as well.

While Renza cleared the table, Silvia disappeared into a back room and returned with a stack of photo albums, large leather-bound volumes that seemed oddly too expensive for the room. She stacked the photo albums in front of me like the next dinner course. They clustered around me—Vivetta, Silvia, Stefano, Paolo and Renza—and led me through the albums.

The photos, as they showed them to me, appeared to flow chronologically. I saw images of receptions and special events, like Vivetta as a young woman at a dance hall with her dashing partner and Paolo's mother's fiftieth wedding anniversary. Vivetta tittered like a schoolgirl as she told me the story of the dance and the man she danced with, the man who became her husband. I saw family vacations to the Alps, when Silvia was just out of diapers and Paolo's hair was jet black. Everyone in the photos smoked. A constant cigarette dangling from Renza and Paolo's lips. Stefano pointed and teased Paolo about his former bad habit.

They moved me through the years, through their lives. Vivetta grew quiet when photos of her dead husband, in the last weeks of his life, appeared on the pages. Then, Silvia cracked an album from a few years back. When I saw the first photo, my breath snagged a bit in my throat. It was an image from my very first trip to Serra, a trip long before the great departure of the ex-wife. The album was my family. My children. My wife.

My daughters were so small then. Both of them had mouths with too many crooked teeth, but that didn't stop them from smiling as they fed Paolo's horse or sat on the memorial in the square, squinting into the sun. And there was my ex-wife, usually caught in mid-translation, her blonde head bent toward the speaker, her eyes tight in concentration. And the nose. The Parenti nose.

Didn't they understand that they were showing me photos of something that no longer existed, of something that had imploded during the intervening years? I thought of a photo I'd seen of Guilfoil with his crew, how he knelt and flexed at the camera, trying to look older than he really was. He was never that way again. And I would never be in a picture like that again, with my two little girls draped around me and my wife with one of her long, tan arms circling my shoulder. They didn't understand. These were pictures before the crash landing. I wasn't supposed to see these.

My ex-wife looked so happy when she wasn't trying to translate conversations. She was excited to be discovering her past. I was happy, too, hanging mostly on the fringes of the pictures, doing what I usually did—observing and making mental notes that I'd transcribe later.

Renza said she had a photo in her computer of me and the girls and the ex-wife in Disneyworld. She said she'd always wanted to go to Florida and Disneyworld. I tried my best to keep from crying. I'm sure if anyone noticed my eyes and the way I coughed to keep my nose clear, it would be Stefano. He was closest to me in age. Maybe he understood, somehow.

Thankfully, it came to an end, the pages of photos of the family I used to have. The limoncello mercifully appeared while I closed the album. I threw back a couple of cold shots. Then, the evening took another twist.

Scott Gould

Like a pair of Santa Clauses, Silvia and Renza disappeared down the hall and returned with their arms full. They gave me a several small bags of wedding *confetti*, tiny bundles of candy that each of the guests would receive at Silvia's wedding. They presented me with three cross-stitched bags, little pouches, emblazoned with a double S ("*Per Silvia e Stefano*," Vivetta explained, in case I missed the significance). The bags were for guests, but they said I could have one, and each of my daughters could have one as well. Then, they brought out two pocketbooks for my girls, ones they'd purchased at the street market in Serra, I guessed. I was working without a translator. And finally, they gave me a printed invitation to Silvia and Stefano's wedding in a couple of weeks.

Now, *they* were crying. I'd come to Serra at the completely wrong time. No wonder Renza rarely smiled. She was spending her nights cross-stitching tiny bags. Her house was covered in scaffolding, her yard littered with empty stucco buckets and stiff, discarded brushes. I looked at Stefano. Through the cloud of smoke, I recognized the dazed expression of a man who had been rolled over by his own wedding plans.

Suddenly, I was enveloped in hugs. Silvia and Renza and Vivetta wrapped their arms around me. They cried harder, releasing that strange combination of stress and joy that weddings and unexpected guests can bring. A new marriage was on the brink of existence. I'd just seen pictures of an old one that had died. I didn't know what to feel. Guilfoil had crashed here and his burned body had been resurrected and given peace on the hillside.

Maybe I was on the way to finding peace as well. I wasn't on fire, but I had come to rest in Serra. That was part of my story now.

CENTOOTTO.

That night, another thunderstorm tumbled down the valley. You could hear it coming from minutes away, the quick blast of lightning and the thunder that ricocheted off the mountainsides. It was late, probably around two or three in the morning, but I went to the door of the Farfagliana and stood beneath the overhang, watching the water rush through the village in the ancient stone gutters. Across the square, in flashes of light, Paolo's house looked like a movie set, the web of scaffolding gleaming in the white flashes. There was a light on in his house, too, high up on the third floor. I wondered if Vivetta was having a restless night after seeing the photos of her dead husband. Or maybe Silvia was unable to sleep with wedding plans crackling through her head, not unlike the lightning. Or perhaps Renza was cross-stitching bags for wedding guests. It was comforting to know someone else was up.

Across the street, I saw the pay phone shining in the storm. I had some minutes left on a phone card. If I was writing this story as fiction—or better yet, if this was my own little movie—I would run across the wet street in the rain and make a phone call. I would punch in the numbers for my ex-wife's new house and I would listen for the connection. The rain would soak me down. (Sure, the symbolism is a little heavy-handed. Me, standing in the rain, being washed clean after all I'd learned in Serra.) She would answer. Even better, *he* would answer and ask who was calling. Maybe I'd say something in Italian, something he couldn't understand, but could only repeat to this wife, who would be too ashamed to translate. Maybe *pene trafitto*. Italian for pierced penis.

I stayed dry, standing in the doorway, watching the silhouette of Serra pop into view with every split second of lightning. I didn't need to call anybody.

CENTONOVE.

Giampiero's English was limited to a head nod. He was one of those rare Europeans who knew absolutely zero English, not a word. I found this utterly admirable. He had closed himself off from the shrink-wrapping of the world and in his tiny village, he remained wonderfully ignorant of things that happened down the mountain, or in another hemisphere.

He was a stately-looking man, with a face that suggested he owned property or art. But he didn't. He owned a tiny house that, rather than clinging to the hillside, sat in the middle of the village, on a small side alley I had failed to notice during the three weeks.

Inside Giampiero's house, the air was cold and dank, like a root cellar. His kitchen was gray and chilly. I felt as though I had stepped into a time warp. The stove was a wood burning contraption, hulking and sooty. The sink appeared to be something you could move in a hurry, with no sense of permanence about it. I didn't see a refrigerator. And the fireplace was wide and deep, almost too big for the room.

I had no translator, so Giampiero and I used hand signals and single words. He knew why I was in Serra; Paolo had briefed him about me, and I—with my bloated American ego—was sure the whole village had dissected my every move.

I tried to ask Giampiero about the airplane. I said, as best I could in Italian, that I'd heard he owned a piece of the crashed Rhomar. He ran a hand across his bald head. His fingers were padded with permanent calluses, so I knew that he'd spent his working years doing something hard, something manual. He was, I assumed, well into his retirement, maybe living by himself. I didn't see any evidence of a woman anywhere in the kitchen.

With the hand not on his head, he pointed to the fireplace, then reached in and grabbed a sooty piece of metal. It was heavy, I could tell, but I was still surprised at the weight when he handed it to me. The two-foot long section, with its u-joint on one end, was as dense a metal as I'd ever held. Giampiero reached across and plinked the surface with his fingernail, amused by the low note it made. It must have weighed twenty pounds. Giampiero made a plane-shape with his hands, then pantomimed a landing. He pointed underneath, trying to tell me that the metal in my hands was part of the landing gear.I also think I heard the word for *grandfather*, so my guess was that Granddaddy somehow came away with a hunk of landing gear. He gestured toward the fireplace again, to the entire back wall of it. I saw a square of charred metal with a couple of rows of ancient rivets. It had to be a section of the fuselage. A tiny chill went through me. This was as close as I'd come to something Guilfoil had actually touched. It was one thing to tromp around an overgrown crash site, emptied of any remnant of the plane, and completely another to see and feel pieces of the Rhomar some six decades later. I stared at the fuselage firewall, hypnotized.

Giampiero wanted me to take photos of him with the piece of landing gear. He said I could use his picture in my magazine. I had no clue how he came to the conclusion I was a magazine reporter. He held the metal piece like a trophy while I clicked away. We were out in the street, at the entrance to the alley, so I could get some sun in the picture. Several villagers peered at us from their benches and doorways. Giampiero waved at each one, and several of the on-lookers rolled their eyes. It was hard to tell what they thought of him, if he was perhaps the village jester, the crazy man who lived in the cave in the middle of town.

When I had enough pictures, I began to thank Giampiero, and he insisted we share a beer. It was maybe eight-thirty in the morning. "*Una birra*," he said, grabbing my arm and pulling me through the alley.

Inside his house, he ducked down a tiny staircase I hadn't noticed earlier, leading to, I guessed, a cellar. Giampiero emerged with two dusty, cold bottles of Moretti. He popped the caps off using the rough edge of the table and slid a bottle down to me. "*Salute*," he said. "*Alla Rhomar, eh?*"

It was probably not the first time Guilfoil's plane had been toasted, but it felt new to me. The beer bit as it went down. Giampiero saw my eyes watering. "*Ah, va bene*," he said and patted me on the shoulder like a friend.

CENTODIECI.

Giampiero is twelve, too young to join the procession gathering in the square. Men with hammers and pry bars, with knives they would normally use for slaughtering animals or chopping stakes for their small gardens. Women, their heads wrapped against the October breezes, stand with the men, some of them ready to steer carts down the path to the selva dell'apparecchio. They have already named the place the plane crashed. Less than two days have passed since it dropped from the sky, and the plane has a history already.

The procession grows slightly as the minutes go by, men and women appearing from between houses, walking down the narrow stone streets beyond the church, carrying homemade baskets and burlap sacks. Giampiero watches as his father talks to Alvaro. He thinks they are speaking about the funeral, because his father keeps pointing up the road, in the direction of the cemetery. Everyone has heard about the funeral.

They have already put the American flyer in the ground, in the corner of the cemetery where the shade covers the graves all day. The funeral happened quickly, before anyone could come up with arguments against burying an American. It was simple, too. The priest, an altar boy, Alvaro and Roberto and maybe a dozen villagers watched Guilfoil disappear into the ground. From the road outside the cemetery two local Fascists spied to make sure Guilfoil didn't suddenly leap to life, a resurrected spy sent to stand in the way of Mussolini and the Nazis.

Without really talking about it, the people in the village

know they cannot return to the plane until Guilfoil is in the ground. The plane is Guilfoil's gift to them, so they must first pay him respect, in exchange for such a valuable present. But they must hurry. They want to get to the plane before the Germans, before the Fascists. The plane belongs to Serra. They accepted it from the sky.

The procession begins its slow march into the selva dell'apparecchio, a line of drab coats and fading dresses. The war has made everyone move slower, but perhaps steadier. No one notices Giampiero following behind, far enough back to hide behind the trees lining the path. The wooden wheels of the carts clack against the rocks that have washed into the ruts. Women talk without moving their hands. Past the washing spring with its flat, beaten-on rocks, deeper into the trees. Giampiero's grandfather is somewhere in the middle of the procession. The men smoke cigarettes down to their fingers. They wonder if they will find cigarettes, perfect American cigarettes, on the plane. Do men fly with extra cigarettes? they ask. Giampiero smells the tobacco from his hiding places. He pretends he is stalking cinghiale the way his father does every winter after the first snow.

A canopy of chestnut trees hangs over the path and captures everything: the blown smoke, the sounds, the smells of the bodies in the procession. Giampiero closes his eyes and sees everything. When he opens them, the people are out of sight, and he scrambles through the trees to reel them back in. When he catches up to the procession, the group has stopped in front of the downed plane.

The size of it steals his breath away. It is the monster in the forest, a creature come to earth. He expects it to make noise, to groan from pain, from lying on its side for too long.

The women begin on the inside, removing what isn't attached, anything that shook loose in the lazy, circular path to the trees and anything that can be unstrapped or cut away. Parachute silks will make baby clothes and white curtains. Strips of leather from seat cushions will become belts.

The men hammer and pry metal away from the skin of the fuselage. The pieces peel off in large squares that Giampiero's father and the others load onto carts. Once they are full, mules and donkeys tow the carts up the narrow pathway toward Serra. They remove the engine cowling and find tiny, intricate pieces of metal that will become children's mysterious toys at Christmas or new latches on the garden gate. The rubber hoses are a complete mystery. No one in Serra has ever seen a hose before. A man, Alvaro's friend, exhales a lungful of cigarette smoke into one end of the hose, just to see if it's hollow. A plume of white exits the opposite end, two feet away, and Alvaro's friend is suddenly a magician, asked to repeat his trick again and again. He laughs, his eyes wide and alive in the afternoon light.

They work until dark, leaving the plane half-skinned. The last cart meanders up the hill toward the village. They return the next day and quit before dark, because of boredom or disinterest. For days after, the procession makes its way down the mountain, each time with fewer and fewer members. They return until there is no reason to come back, until there is no metal to salvage, no rivets to struggle with. In a couple of weeks, the plane has disappeared. In the selva dell'apparecchio, it no longer appears as though a plane crashed. Rather, the scar in the chestnut trees is a scene of decay, only an imprint of a plane in the earth, a quiet reminder of its former life.

The metal the families can't use is taken down the mountain to Pistoia and sold to a company that manufactures mess kits for the Italian army. Soon, an Italian soldier somewhere will be eating food he doesn't want from the remains of an American B-17. Giampiero's father uses one piece of the fuselage to line the small fireplace in their house, and a couple of pieces of landing gear serve as fireplace irons, where Giampiero's mother balances pots of white beans above the coals.

Giampiero will live in that house until he dies, lighting fires, the heat and light reflected by the skin of the plane.

CENTOUNDICI.

I was packed, my body-bag sized duffel already shoved into the trunk of the VW, and I found myself with a little time to kill before I headed down the mountain and toward Florence. The village was beginning to wake up. I heard children yelling in the houses tucked off the main street. Sonia rolled up the door of her store and a new guy, one I didn't recognize, hosed off the front stoop of the café. The sun breeched the tops of the buildings, and the bench in front of the Farfagliana was bathed in morning sun. I sat for a minute until I got restless, and when the latest dose of Lortab kicked in, I decided to walk to the cemetery.

The cemetery sat surrounded by a copse of cedars and chestnuts, just on the outskirts of the village. A high cement wall encircled the graves, but I'd been told the gate was never locked. I mean, there was an actual lock, a huge one, but it hung there uselessly. I walked to the back corner of the site, which was still cool in the shade. This corner, Daniele told me, was where Guilfoil lay a year or so, until an American military detail liberated the village, exhumed the body and shipped him home.

In that corner, it was as quiet as it should have been, the only sounds a whisper of breeze in the branches and a bird angry with me for intruding. I was glad I had come to Guilfoil's place in Serra before I left. I had not avoided it on purpose. I just didn't think it would be valuable. He wasn't there that long. And where he'd lain was now covered with other graves, probably more elaborate than his had ever been. But this felt appropriate. I hadn't come to know Guilfoil personally on my trip. That was never the point. I'd come, rather, to hear the stories that swirled around Guilfoil, the things that happened because he'd crashed into the trees on a hillside. My old writing teacher would call Guilfoil's crash the catalytic event of the narrative. I came in search of how these people kept Guilfoil's tale alive, to look for the stories that orbited him. That's what I wanted to hear.

I wondered about my own catalytic event. Was it the sandals? The trip to Italy years back? Something buried long before the trip that I couldn't recall? If there was a single, striking occurrence that caused a marriage to dissolve, I could have spotted it and corrected the wrong. (I could have beat the clock.) But the fact of the matter was, there was never a single turn of the worm. That was the difference between Guilfoil and me. His crash began some stories. My crash ended them. He died. I didn't. I'm supposed to be the lucky one.

I walked back to Serra and sat on the bench. I wasn't the only one enjoying the morning, a morning that seemed cooler and washed clean by the storm the night before. Giampiero waved from his seat across the street, where he talked with one of the masons working on Paolo's house. Perhaps he was telling him about my visit earlier that morning. Stefano pulled by in a tiny Fiat, the cab already hazy with cigarette smoke. A card game was about to begin at the wicker table. The sour woman swept the war memorial like she was on a mission, the broom whisking loudly across the stones.

The sun grew brighter, so bright I could barely see my watch. It was time to leave. I'd made my goodbyes with Paolo's family the night before, so there was no one left to hug. I didn't notice the sound of the broom cease. I stared at my sandals—my divorce sandals—and tried to adjust to the glare, when something passed between me and the sun. The shadow stayed put, blocking the light. I looked up. It was the sour woman, leaning slightly on her broom handle. It was the closest I'd been to her. Her eyes, which I'd always assumed to be dark and menacing, were actually light-colored. They almost sparkled. The lines at their corners grew tighter, as if she was straining under an effort of some kind. She had half a smile on her lips. It would have been a whole one, but she was trying to say something to me.

I beat her to it. "*Buon giorno*," I said quickly, giving it my best Italian lilt. "*Come stai?*" It was as if she didn't even hear me. Her complete focus was on the words she was about to say.

She cleared her throat and said, very formally, in gorgeous, measured English, "And good morning. Travel well." I smiled and nodded. I think I may have said "Ah" or something. I don't recall. What I do remember is the expression on her face. It was the look a fifth grader gets when she answers a math problem correctly, that strange mixture of relief and pride. There above me, she beamed. "Travel well," she said again and turned back toward the monument, using the broom as a make-shift cane.

A wave of something flowed over me, not sadness exactly, but a feeling akin to gratitude tinged with a deep sympathy. I imagined the woman finding the right English words to say and practicing them in her house, waiting for the time to speak to me. She'd found the perfect moment, my last moment in Serra, to accept me.

I had nothing. I had not discovered some mystery about Guilfoil, I had not bedded a bank teller or ruined the reputation of my ex-wife, but I had convinced an old Italian woman that I meant no harm, that I was only chasing down stories, some hers, some mine.

Suddenly, there was no one in the world to be angry with.

CENTODODICI.

Guilfoil perches on a thick chestnut branch, wedged in the crook near the trunk. Below him, in the shady corner of the cemetery, he is committed to the earth. He hears the word over and over in Italian. Commit. Commettere.

The priest is a tiny soft man who looks out of place in the open air. The voice that comes from his mouth doesn't seem to belong to him—it's so large and formal, filling the air above the hole in the ground. Guilfoil doesn't know Italian, other than the words for beautiful and beer. But he feels the translation for the word commit. The word buzzes in his ear. He is being committed. Here. In this little cemetery that smells like incense and autumn.

So, he thinks, this is what happens when it happens. You get to watch yourself lowered in the strange soil, get to watch a small crowd of solemn people commit you to a tiny piece of their village, blowing in their hands to ward off the cold. They are giving me title to this piece of dirt, Guilfoil thinks.

Guilfoil has never owned anything he could stand on.

From his spot in the tree, Guilfoil can see over the cemetery wall. A dark car—a model Guilfoil doesn't recognize, not a Ford or a Mercury—sits just outside the gate, exhaust puffing smoke signals from its back end. A man in a uniform peers through the bars of the gate, making sure the villagers are not plotting and scheming with a dead man.

Guilfoil cannot see his body below. It is inside a simple box, a coffin made of a wood he doesn't recognize, too dark to be pine. Guilfoil thinks the men outside the gate might demand to search the coffin before it is committed, but they seem afraid to cross the cemetery gates. The idea of that much death so close to them is a dark omen for the rest of the day, or the rest of the war. Guilfoil wants to tell them not to worry, that death has nothing to do with portents and planning, that death is the most random eventuality in the world. Two inches to the left and Guilfoil would have been alive and dangling from a parachute, just another falling angel, drifting into chestnut trees in the valley. Now, he sits, committed to be dead forever.

The first shovelful of dirt on the wood sounds like a quick, tight drum roll. Except for the two men assigned to fill the hole, the small crowd evaporates. Several of them pause at the markers of relatives or friends, crossing themselves and mumbling a quick, quiet prayer. They shoulder by the men at the gates, who refuse to move completely out of the way. These are men who survive on suspicion, and they are sure a plot will still break out when they are not looking. They do not understand why the village would want to taint their cemetery with the body of an American, an American who is probably a Methodist or a Lutheran. They do not understand what it means to commit. Commettere.

Guilfoil likes his tree. The branch feels solid under him, so different than his seat in the plane that was held up by nothing but moving air. He will sit there for months, watch the snow drape the headstones when winter comes, watch the bees begin to work the chestnut flowers when the weather warms. He will not be prepared for the day when the Americans arrive in the summer, to dig up what's left of him and take it back to Chicago. They will never remove all of Guilfoil. Some part of him stays, remains high above Serra's cemetery, in the chestnut tree watching and listening to the village around him grow older.

Time will pass. In the selva dell'apparecchio, the trees will continue to grow, some of them sprouting new shoots out of the burned trunks. There is no sign of the plane. A man hunting funghi will scan the woods with a metal detector and find nothing among the briars and brush. Adriana will grow bent, her sight failing each season, but still able to spot angels in the valley when she gazes off the balcony of her

Scott Gould

summer home. One big-headed man, a Parenti, will tell visitors who bother to listen that Guilfoil was buried just off the road to the selva dell'apparecchio, under a tiny, antique Fiat. He will be wrong and confused by the years. Guilfoil will continue to fade as people die. Giampiero will almost recall him when he lights a fire before dawn in the winter dark. Roberto will have a flash of memory when he smells the first smoky fires in autumn, when his neighbor roasts racks of chestnuts in the metato. Just a flash and no more.

They never realize Guilfoil is always there, still whispering in their ears when they least expect it, telling them what it is like to fly in circles and drift into trees below Serra, what is it like to commit himself to people who care for the dead so far from home.

Guilfoil eventually went home. So did I. When I landed, it wasn't Independence Day—that had already passed—but I felt freed. There was a moment I wanted to feel like a failure for not exacting some kind of grand revenge. It wouldn't have been the first time I returned from Italy thinking I had come up short. But this time, the sense of not accomplishing something was fleeting. I wondered if Guilfoil had the same sense when he finally realized the plane was going down and he couldn't do a thing about it. Or even if he had that moment of clarity. Maybe I was lucky. I had survived the crash. I was going home alive.

I drove back into town and my daughters were waiting for me at the house on Stono Avenue, the house that was too big for me. Everything seemed to have grown while I'd been away—my daughters, the grass, the house itself. The girls had somehow added years to their faces in just a few weeks. They both looked like college students, home on a break. For the first time in years, it didn't twist my heart to look at their faces and see their mother's eyes staring back at me.

They wanted to know what I'd brought them, how I was feeling, if I was tired from all the travel. I reached into my bag and pulled out t-shirts I bought from the vendors in the square and little trinkets from my short trip to the coast. I showed them my journal stuffed with beer labels I'd soaked off bottles. And I gave them the pocketbooks and little cross-stitched pouches from Renza and Silvia.

"You don't know, do you?" I said. "Silvia is getting married. Here's an invitation." I passed the card to them and they immediately wanted to know about Silvia's fiancé.

I launched into the story about Stephano and his cigarettes. That led me to tell them about the renovations at Paolo's house and the apartment I lived in and the swallows outside the window and my trip to the little forest of the machine. I forgot how tired I was. I couldn't stop talking. I told my daughters about Guilfoil and the cemetery, about the food at Zacco, about the Italian Bank Teller (which made them roll their eyes and shake their heads). I told them about the Lortab dreams I dreamed. I told them about the old woman who broomed the War Memorial every morning. They listened to every word.

I told them all the stories I could recall, all of the ones I brought back from Serra, and I think that may have been the best gift I've ever given them.

AN EPILOGUE

I am six-foot-three and my hairline is hauling ass.

I quit taking the Lortab the week after I returned from Serra because I was beginning to enjoy it too much. I miss the dreams, though. Once a week, I go to Tito's for pizza, so I can hear the owner speak Italian. Tito still calls me *autore* every time I walk in the door and he always brags about how big the lemons are in Naples. My ex-wife married and divorced the husband with the jewelry junk. I take very little joy in that. He was always good material for a story.

I don't like to date, but I try with varying degrees of success. I was engaged for a bit, to Sharon from the Lyle Lovett concert. I discovered that her flitting and fluttering in and out of conversations was also the strategy she employed in regard to engagements. She flitted and fluttered away for good one day, but I got the ring back.

I sold the big house on Stono Avenue and left the pergola behind. My new kitchen is narrow and very small, so small that it's hard to have a conversation in it, good or bad. I cycle obsessively, and even though I'm a big person, I love to pedal up mountains and pretend I am in Italy, climbing the switchbacks between Panicagliora and Serra, pretend I am one of the old men in the cycling club, stamping out a rhythm on the pedals.

I still love my job. I love my daughters, love watching them grow up. I can talk on the phone with my ex-wife without feeling my heart flip and land awkwardly in my gut.

The Surdna Foundation liked my little essay about Guilfoil and the people in Serra and what might have gone on in his head. (They had no questions about anything.) I think about Guilfoil often and toy with the idea of trying to hunt down some of his family in Chee-ka-goes, but I chicken out when I rehearse what I would say if they answered the phone. I still do that—rehearse dialogue ahead of time.

I sit on the front porch of my new, tiny house just before dusk and drink cheap beer and watch frantic swallows fly crazy circles around the chimney across the street. I hope they are keeping the mosquitoes away.

I wonder if they somehow recognize me, if somehow they've heard of me. I wonder if they can see I'm happy where I am.

I am considering flying lessons.

Acknowledgements

I owe an immense debt to the fine people of Serra Pistoiese, Italy...To those who translated for me, laughed with me, drank with me, fed me, pointed me in the right directions—I thank you and hope our paths cross soon. Special thanks to Paolo, Renza and Silvia for welcoming me time and again. Thanks to the Surdna Foundation; they (ultimately) received a great deal more than they bargained for, I suppose. Thanks to Dr. Burnikel, who replaced the knee. Thanks to Antonluigi Aiazzi for the gift of Guilfoil. (I hope the two of them are somewhere, flying.) Many thanks to the folks at Vine Leaves Press, especially Jessica Bell, Amie McCracken and Melanie Faith. (Melanie's keen eye and rock solid instincts truly gave this book its shape. Much thanks to her.) A special note of gratitude to Bret Lott. Thanks as always to my fishing partner, Jack Gould. Thanks to my daughters, who understand what it's like to have a storyteller for a father. And finally, thanks to Shannon for support that never wavers.

A portion of this memoir was excerpted in *Crazyhorse*, Number 93.

VINE LEAVES PRESS

Enjoyed this book?
Go to *vineleavespress.com* to find more.

CPSIA information can be obtained
at www.ICGtesting.com
Printed in the USA
LVHW040024180721
692994LV00008B/64